A Primer of
Infant Development

A Series of Books in Psychology

Editors: Richard C. Atkinson
Jonathan Freedman
Gardner Lindzey
Richard F. Thompson

T. G. R. Bower

University of Edinburgh

A Primer of
Infant Development

W. H. Freeman and Company
San Francisco

Library of Congress Cataloging in Publication Data

Bower, T. G. R. 1941–
   A primer of infant develompent.

   Bibliography: p.
   Includes index.
   1. Infant psychology.   I. Title.
BF723.I6B624   155.4'22   76-27827
ISBN 0-7167-0499-4
ISBN 0-7167-0498-6 pbk.

Printed in the United States of America

9 8 7 6 5 4 3 2 1

Contents

Preface

Few would dissent from the proposition that infancy is the most critical period of human development, the period in which the basic frameworks for later development are established. Despite this, it is only recently that we have been able to investigate what goes on during infancy. The explosion of information that has occurred in all aspects of development during this period is truly astounding and bewildering in its complexity. My purpose in writing this book is to summarize such data and put it into a context that would help all those intimately concerned with babies and their development. If I have succeeded in conveying the needs and abilities of babies, as we now see them, I shall feel well rewarded.

This book is one of a triad I wrote while a fellow at the Center for Advanced Study in the Behavioral Sciences. I cannot thank the Center enough for providing me with the most stimulating and nurturant academic environment I have known. I would particularly like to thank Agnes Paige, who turned my manuscripts into beautiful typescripts.

Here, too, I must acknowledge a special debt to Jane Dunkeld Turnbull and Jennifer G. Wishart for their comprehensive and invaluable assistance.

T. G. R. Bower

A Primer of
Infant Development

1　The Study of Infancy

Infancy is that brief period of human life which precedes the use of language. Despite its short duration, infancy is viewed by many as the most critical segment of life, the period in which basic developmental pathways are laid down for all human skills and thought processes. Until fairly recently, however, the origin of these human attributes and the manner in which they evolve were more a matter of speculation than science. There were simply very few methods available for studying what infants are capable of doing or perceiving or knowing at various ages. It is only in the last few years that new experimental techniques have provided us with a means of asking more precise questions of infants—and many of the answers we have received have been surprising. This new information has also raised some new and intriguing questions.

An infant is literally someone who does not talk. Infancy is thus that period of life which begins at birth and ends with the beginning of language use. The normal duration of infancy, in this strict sense, is about eighteen months. It may seem strange to devote a whole book, even a small book, to such a short segment of human life. Why should 2 percent of a lifespan merit such attention? There are various answers to this, all valid. Probably more of the skills that separate human beings from other animals are acquired in infancy than in all the rest of childhood together. By the end of infancy the baby is sociable and cooperative. He has learned what is necessary for language, possibly the most important of all human skills. He can walk on his own two feet. He has the refined manual skills that man shares with no other animal. He can use tools to a limited extent, but an extent greater than any nonhuman. He has acquired some very basic and important concepts—concepts of space, causality, number. All this has happened in eighteen months, grown from what look like most unpromising beginnings.

The Importance of Infancy

If infancy is the busiest period of development, it is also, according to many theorists, the most sensitive period. Untoward experiences in infancy are supposed to have permanent effects on all subsequent development. Lack of those experiences normal to infancy is claimed to prevent normal development.

Consider the influential theory offered by Erik Erikson. During infancy, according to Erikson, the baby forms either a basic trust of the world or a basic mistrust of the world:

> Mothers create a sense of trust in their children by that kind of administration which in its quality combines sensitive care of the baby's individual needs and a firm sense of personal trustworthiness within the trusted framework of their culture's life style.[1]

Deviations from such a style, a mother who is unpredictable or inattentive, are supposed to create a basic mistrust which can last throughout the rest of the individual's life.

The way the mother treats her teething baby is considered an especially critical want. According to Erikson, the pain of teething can be relieved only by biting. The mother has always relieved the baby's pain before, particularly the pain of hunger, and now she does not allow him to bite her. Hence, in a sense, she is violating the trust the baby had invested in her. Too severe a violation can, allegedly, lead to basic mistrust.

A second crucial stage, again in infancy, is the one in which the baby acquires either a sense of autonomy or a sense of shame and doubt. Toilet training is supposedly the critical event here:

> Doubt is the brother of shame. Where shame is dependent on the consciousness of being upright and exposed, doubt, so clinical observation leads me to believe, has much to do with a consciousness of having a front and a back—and especially a "behind." For this reverse area of the body,

with its aggressive and libidinal* focus in the sphincters and in the buttocks, cannot be seen by the child, and yet it can be dominated by the will of others. The "behind" is the small being's dark continent, an area of the body which can be magically dominated and effectively invaded by those who would attack one's power of autonomy and who would designate as evil those products of the bowels which were felt to be all right when they were being passed. This basic sense of doubt in whatever one has left behind forms a substratum for later and more verbal forms of compulsive doubting; this finds its adult expression in paranoiac fears concerning hidden persecutors and secret persecutions threatening from behind (and from within the behind).

This stage, therefore, becomes decisive for the ratio of love and hate, cooperation and willfulness, freedom of self-expression and its suppression. From a sense of self-control without loss of self-esteem comes a lasting sense of good will and pride; from a sense of loss of self-control and of foreign overcontrol comes a lasting propensity for doubt and shame.[2]

Erikson's theory is a complex, rich tapestry. Short extracts like those above do not do justice to its detailed patterning. Nonetheless, I think we can understand what Erikson is saying. The formation of basic trust requires that those people who take care of the baby be trustworthy and reliable. The baby must be able to expect consistent responses from those around him if he is to acquire a basic trust of the world. If the baby's caretakers treat him now one way and now another, so that he can form no reliable expectations about what will happen in response to anything he does, then he will grow up with a basic mistrust of the world.

In this framework, we can see why teething is so important an event, particularly for a breast-fed baby. It is probable that the first and most persistent pains to trouble an infant are the pains of hunger. His mother will relieve these pains by feeding him, by giving him her breast to suck. Feeding occurs several times a day, every day of the baby's life. The baby will surely come to associate his mother with consistently reliable relief

---

*The adjective *libidinal* comes from the noun *libido,* which has a complex technical meaning. Erikson defines it as pleasure-seeking urges, which are not sexual at this stage.

from the nagging pains of hunger. But what must happen when budding teeth make their insistent presence unpleasantly felt? The baby will bite, will bite on anything put in his mouth. If it happens to be his mother's breast that he is biting, the consequences will not be relief of pain. They are more likely to be withdrawal of the breast, and probably a scolding.

We can surely share some of the conflict the baby must feel at this point. The person, and the situation, that he has come to rely on most strongly for comfort is suddenly refusing him comfort in a way that must be incomprehensible at first. Only if the baby can discriminate the pains of hunger from the pains of teething, and can learn that the two pains cannot be simultaneously assuaged, will he be able to preserve his basic trust in the world throughout this crisis.

A similar conflict underlies the acquisition of autonomy or doubt. As the baby acquires control of his bowels, he must learn why bowel movement leads sometimes to approval and sometimes to disapproval. The failure to understand why the same behavior can elicit either response is at the root of the toilet-training crisis.

I think we can all understand the nature of the conflict involved. As adults, we are often confronted with situations in which there are two ways of perceiving an event, so that some new discrimination must be made in order to resolve the confusion. Although these are rarely crisis situations for adults, in Erikson's view the infant is so sensitive to such experiences that they have deep and lasting effects on development.

One school of thought, in fact, is that all human skills and abilities evolve through this kind of selection process, as the result of specific encounters with certain types of environmental stimuli. According to this *empiricist* theory, specific inputs from the environment are necessary for development to occur at all. There are, of course, many psychologists who dispute this. The *nativist* argument is that development is biologically determined and the human attributes of each individual emerge as the result of *gene expression*. According to this view, simple growth or maturation of genetically predetermined neural structures is responsible for the emergence of specific human skills and abilities.

Apart from the original concept of "native endowment," the recent explosion of knowledge in genetics has shown how information that is coded in molecular structures within the fertilized egg controls the sequence of chemical events that will result in the development of a complete, complexly differentiated organism. Thus, by extension, all development takes place under genetic control, as a physiological process which is independent of environmental factors. The implication of the nativist viewpoint, of course, is that any individual's potential skills and capacities are fixed at the moment of conception, the point at which a sperm cell enters an ovum, and can be neither enhanced nor diminished by external events.

Infancy has been one of the main areas in which nativists could confront their opponents. This is because the rate of change in infancy is so rapid that it is feasible to look for the effects or lack of effects of experience on some aspect of development. The normal baby, for example, is able to reach quite accurately around the age of five months. It is therefore feasible to provide a group of newborns with special experiences to see whether these experiences accelerate the development of reaching. According to the nativist position, experiences of any sort can do nothing to change the rate of development. Thus such experiments must necessarily fail to produce results. As we shall see, the balance of evidence is against this position—a finding that has implications for the socially more serious nativist claim that adult intelligence is determined by gene expression and is relatively independent of environment.

The Scientific Study of Infancy

I hope the importance and fascination of infancy is clear from the brief outline above. However, an area can be fascinating, yet inaccessible. For many years infancy was like the dark side of the moon. We simply had very few ways of finding out what was going on in the mind of the baby. Babies are extremely charming, but are not typically willing to cooperate with psychologists. Most psychological investigation depends on communication between psychologist and subject, communication that typically relies on language. The very definition of infancy, the period of life prior to language, means that we cannot simply ask babies questions and give them instructions, as with older human beings. We must rely on nonverbal techniques, methods of communication that do not depend on language.

The availability of suitable techniques has determined the kinds of things that psychologists could study. The recent growth in scientific techniques has enabled us to study a wider range of capacities. However, since our knowledge of infancy is limited to the kinds of questions we can investigate, let us begin by discussing the techniques that are available.

The seemingly simplest technique is direct observation of infant behavior in natural situations. For a long time this was the only technique available. It is currently enjoying a re-surgence as part of the so-called ethological approach to human behavior. Ethology is a branch of the study of animal behavior in which animals are observed in their natural surroundings. Instead of looking at laboratory animals in cages, ethologists have pursued their subjects through wood, field, and stream in an endeavor to describe their *natural* behavior, as opposed to the bizarre behaviors one sees in caged animals, deprived of any kind of freedom. There are difficulties with this approach in the case of the human animal, as we shall see.

The descriptions of development that came out of early naturalistic studies were typically statements about the ages at which babies performed certain motor activities. These motor developments were usually, but not always, described in rather wholistic terms, such as reaching, or creeping, or standing. Di-rect observation, particularly at this gross level of analysis, does not permit us to say anything very much about less obvious behaviors. Moreover, this method doesn't tell us much about what the baby might be seeing or hearing or thinking, especially in the first few months of life, when there are few very obvious behaviors to observe.

In recent years the increasing availability of inexpensive videotape recording equipment has enabled researchers to do much more detailed analyses of behavior than were previously possible. The pioneers of this approach were anthropologists.

The lines of research they began have furnished some of the most exciting data currently available, particularly in the areas of communication between mother and infant. This kind of investigation is invaluable and has provided information that is unobtainable by other methods. However, such studies still do not bear forcibly on areas of traditional interest to psychologists—the areas of perceiving, feeling, and thinking.

There have been numerous attempts to use fine-grain motor behavior to analyze these more subtle processes. Sometimes these methods are perfectly satisfactory. In most cases, however, this is only in situations that allow us to make some positive assertion. For example, suppose we show a baby an object and then move it to the right. If the baby looks at the object, and follows it when it moves, smoothly and without error, we can state with certainty that he is able to see the object, can perceive that it has moved to the right, and has sufficient control over his eye muscles to be able to use this information to keep visual contact with the object.

Suppose, though, that when the object moves to the right, the baby looks to the left. Occurrences of this sort of behavior in very young babies have been reported. Does this mean that the baby can't tell the difference between a movement to the right and a movement to the left, or does it mean that he can't control his eye muscles well enough to use the information that is coming in through his eyes? Questions of this sort are always a problem and make it difficult to say what babies *cannot* do. If a baby *can* do something, well and good. If he cannot, finding out why is a major problem.

A second problem with natural-observation techniques lies in the word *natural*. Many of those who use this term assume that if they observe a baby in his own home environment, they are somehow getting at behavior that is biologically more natural or real than would appear in a laboratory situation. This is a strange notion. No human beings live in a natural environment. All human environments have been shaped by man for man's ultimate comfort. They are not natural. Furthermore, the behavior that a baby will produce is very much a function of the particular environment he is in. Simple parameters such as room temperature determine a great deal of what we can see when we observe a baby. Similarly, the conditions of observation affect what the baby will show us of his behavioral repertoire.

An instance of this from my own experience was my introduction to the possibility that very small babies, under four weeks of age, can use their hands and arms. At the time, I was visiting my brother, who had a three-week-old infant. While we were chatting, I heard a bell ringing in the background. I was told that that was the baby playing with his bell. My first reaction was that babies of that age do not play with bells.

Shortly thereafter, a similar phenomenon was demonstrated to me by a professional colleague. At that point I realized that my belief that three-week-old babies do not reach out and play with objects was based on observations of three-week-old babies who had never had anything put within their reach. The simple change in the environment, placing an object within reach, produced a behavior that was completely new to me, quite puzzling, at first seemingly impossible. If there are no things within reach, then of course babies will not reach out. If there are, they will. Which is the natural environment? There is no way we can answer that question. Neither environment is natural in the sense that the environment of a wild animal can be natural. All human environments are made by human beings for human purposes.

Similar problems arise with experimental methods. Consider the ingenious *fixation-preference* technique, a popular method of discovering the perceptual capacities of babies. A baby is shown two different objects or visual displays, one on his right and one on his left, and the time he spends looking at each display is recorded. Then the two displays are switched, and the time the baby spends looking at each display is again recorded. After a few repetitions of this procedure, we have a record of how much time the baby has spent looking at each display. Since both displays have appeared equally often on right and left, we need not worry about the baby simply liking to look to the right, for example. If the baby has spent significantly more time looking at one display than the other, we can conclude that he prefers that display, and therefore that he can tell the two displays apart.[3] This technique has been used to show that very

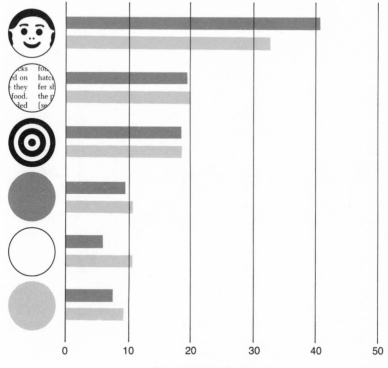

Percent of total fixation time

FIGURE 1.1
This shows the percentage of time babies spent looking at each of the displays on the left. (The last three discs represent plain red, white, and yellow.) The dark bars show the results for babies two to three months old; the light bars represent older babies. (From R. L. Fantz, The origin of form perception. Copyright © 1961 by Scientific American, Inc. All rights reserved.)

small babies are capable of discriminating between displays like those shown in Figure 1.1.

Suppose, though, that the baby shows no preference at all and looks at each display equally often. This might mean that he can't tell the displays apart. It might also well mean that he can tell the displays apart, but simply has no preference. Any conclusion reached in this negative case must be highly tentative. One of the problems in interpreting preference data is that a baby's preferences change with development. It is apparent

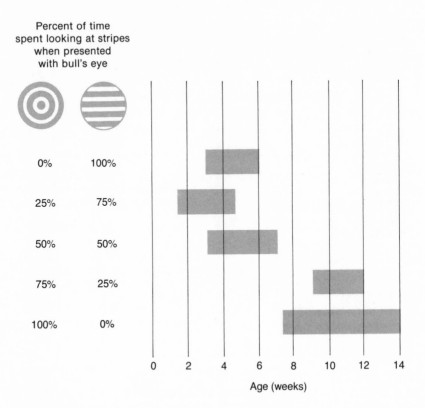

FIGURE 1.2
Changes in preference with age. At around six weeks the average baby shows no preference between the striped pattern and the bull's-eye pattern. Since both younger and older babies do have preferences, but in opposite directions, it would be perilous to assert that at this age the baby is unable to discriminate between the two patterns. (Data from Fantz, 1961.)

from the example in Figure 1.2 that the absence of a particular preference does not necessarily mean that a baby *cannot* tell two things apart.

A somewhat more potent technique for the study of perceptual processes is the *habituation paradigm*. This method requires nothing more from the baby than the capacity to become bored with a repetitive stimulus, a process referred to as *habituation*. This technique has been used, for example, to test the capacity of infants to discriminate speech sounds.[4] The baby is placed in a dimly lit room, with nothing to look at and not really enough light for him to see anything anyway. A loudspeaker off to one side then begins to produce the sound *pa-pa . . . pa-pa . . . pa-pa.* The baby (provided he has not fallen asleep) will typically turn toward the sound. His heart rate will also change. Both these signals indicate that the baby is attending to the sound. After some time he becomes habituated to the repetitive *pa-pa* sound. His heart rate returns to normal, and he shows no further interest in the loudspeaker. The sound changed to *ta-ta . . . ta-ta . . . ta-ta.* In the actual study there was again, at this point, a change in the baby's heart rate and he again turned toward the loudspeaker, showing that he had detected the change in the sound.

The habituation paradigm is a very useful technique, since it can be applied to discriminations in any area of perception. It is all too easy to bore babies with repetitive stimuli, so that virtually any type of stimulus can be used. In fact, the only major limitation of this technique is that the baby's habituation to a situation may become chronic, so that he blanks out the whole input and for this reason fails to notice the changes, even changes we know he can detect.

A variant of the habituation paradigm, called the *surprise paradigm,* has been developed to allow deeper probing into the baby's perceptual processes. In the habituation paradigm we introduce a stimulus and leave it on long enough for the baby to discover all the features of it that he can. We then change some features of this stimulus. If it is a feature that the baby has been able to register, we can expect to see the kind of orienting behavior described above. The cause of this orienting behavior is presumably an awareness that some apparently constant feature of the environment has changed.

The point to note is that with the habituation paradigm we are introducing a regularity, the original stimulus, into the baby's world. The surprise paradigm, by contrast, relies on regularities that exist in the world anyway. We simply present the baby with an impossible event. If he recognizes that the event is impossible, we should see some indication of surprise, more than if we present him with a possible event.

An example of this paradigm is an experiment devised by Aronson and Rosenbloom.[5] A mother sits facing her baby, with a soundproof glass screen between them. The baby can see her, but her voice is projected through a stereo system. The stereo system can be adjusted so as to make the mother's voice seem to come from her mouth, or from any other point in space. Now, of course, voices normally come from mouths, not from some point several feet to the right or left of the mouth. If the infant has detected this regularity in the world, the displaced voice presentation should surprise him. It did, in fact, produce this result in babies older than three weeks or so.

Attempts have been made to use the technique to get at more complex levels of understanding. For example, if the support is pulled from under an object, the object normally falls down. Suppose we present an infant with this event and with an impossible event, in which the unsupported object simply floats in mid air (Figure 1.3). If the infant has detected the environ-

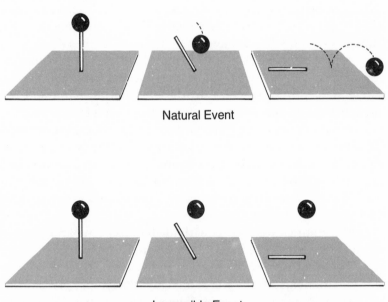

Natural Event

Impossible Event

FIGURE 1.3
The natural consequence of gravity is that the ball will fall when the stick on which it was balanced falls over. Not until the second half-year of life are babies more surprised by the second sequence of events than they are by the first one.

mental regularity that unsupported objects fall down, then the latter event should be more surprising than the former. In fact it is, but not for infants of less than nine months or so. It seems to take nine months for this regularity to be detected.

The Limits of Experimentation

The experimental methods we have discussed are techniques for assessing the *capacities* of babies of various ages. As you will have noticed, describing these capacities is difficult enough, particularly when we move away from the relatively simple levels of perception mentioned above. When it comes to the developmental process itself, the problem of investigation becomes much more complex. At one extreme is the nativist position that all capacities emerge as a consequence of gene expression, and that practice, experience, reward and punishment, all the standard psychological forces, are quite irrelevant. At the opposite extreme, the empiricist maintains that specific inputs from the environment are necessary for development to take place; without these inputs, the baby will remain a helpless, if ever bigger, baby. These are the two simplest possible accounts of development. Simple as they are, it is hard to find a decisive test between them.

For example, one clear test of the nativist hypothesis would be to isolate a baby from all possible inputs from the environment. Theoretically, the baby should be normal when returned to the world. Such an experiment is obviously immoral and could never be performed. However, psychologists have tried to find close approximations to this situation, either by going to cultures in which infants are more restricted than in our own or by studying infants who are restricted for some medical reason.

The most extreme instance of this is an infant described by Wolff.[6] This infant suffered from arrhinencephaly, a disorder in which inputs from the environment simply could not reach the brain as signals, but were completely blocked by the "noise" produced by the disorder. In spite of this, the baby did develop some behaviors in her short life. She became able to lift her head, roll over, and even make incipient locomotor movements.

It is no great catalog, but these abilities were acquired without any support from the environment at all. A strong-minded nativist might argue from this case that other capacities would have appeared without environmental support if the baby had not had the disorder which disabled her.

One might think that the empiricist case would be easier to test. In fact, it is more complicated than it seems. In an ideal experiment, the effect of a particular environmental input would be tested by providing it to one group of babies and withholding it from another group. In theory, the babies in the first group should make the developmental step in question; those in the second group should not. Such an experiment, if it were feasible, would also be immoral. We cannot purposely impose a condition that would retard the development of a baby. In fact, there is a similar moral question involved in accelerating normal development. The issue of the amount of control that one can apportion to oneself in experimentation with human beings is far from resolved. And even if this issue were resolved, there is still the practical problem of getting control. Many of the great, socially approved adventures in environmental manipulation have failed simply because of lack of control. A child is alive for 24 hours a day. Not even the most ambitious intervention program has attempted to control more than a fraction of that time.

For all these reasons, a perhaps undue amount of effort has gone into descriptions of the newborn human. The newborn has just emerged from the tranquility of the womb, a world in which there are no rewards, no punishments, no frustrations, no conflicts. Any abilities he has at this point are purely the result of genetic expression. He has had no experience that could shape any behavior or skill or concept. This is why the world of the newborn is so critical in all accounts of development. We will consider this fascinating enigma in the next chapter.

2 The World of the Newborn

The newborn baby has just begun his psychological life. Prior to birth he has experienced no rewards or punishments, successes or failures, none of the psychological forces that might produce learning. Has the newborn any developed behaviors, then? One important psychological theory would say no. The casual observer would probably say no, as well. Despite this, the newborn is indeed a competent creature. He has a functioning perceptual system, some motor skills, and a truly astonishing repertoire of social behaviors, behaviors for interacting with people. In addition, the newborn can learn very efficiently. Immediately after birth all these capacities are put to use; for example, the infant of a few days can be said to have learned to identify his mother.

The human newborn must rank as one of the most fascinating organisms with which psychologists ever work. A newborn baby has just emerged from the completely safe, completely stable, tranquil world of the womb into a world of conflicts and contradictions—the normal psychological environment of human beings. Scientific fascination with the newborn lies in the fact that prior to birth there has been no psychological environment, no way in which any known process of learning could create any skills or knowledge whatsoever. Any capacity that the baby has at the moment of birth must therefore be innate, a result of genetic expression in a physical and chemical environment.

The scientific interest in the newborn is perhaps matched only by his human interest. The baby is so vulnerable and yet so appealing, a source of wonder and sometimes apprehension, to his parents. The questions that parents ask are very similar to the questions that scientists ask: Can the baby see? Can he hear? Does he know what's going on? Does he know his mother, his father? Not long ago the answer given to all these questions would have been no. To the casual eye, the newborn baby seems as helpless and uncapable a creature as one could find. From all outward appearances, he can do nothing except eat and sleep and cry.

The casual eye, in this case, as in so many cases, is completely wrong. The human newborn is perhaps as capable a young organism as any in the whole of the animal kingdom. He has some abilities that surpass those of any other primate, some that may, in fact, surpass the same abilities in older members of his species. One of these, which complicates the scientific problem immensely, is the newborn's capacity for learning. Previously it seemed that one of the scientific charms of the newborn was that he gave us unparalleled opportunities to find out just how much structure, capacity, or knowledge could be built in without benefit of any psychological environment. The fact that newborns can learn, and begin to do so the minute they emerge from the womb, makes the task of separating innate abilities from acquired ones very much more complex.

The Learning Ability of Newborns

For a long time there was controversy over whether or not newborns could learn at all. That controversy is pretty much resolved. Indeed, one expert on newborn learning has gone so far as to say that newborns can learn better on the first day of life than they ever will be able to again.[1] Consider a very simple learning experiment in which newborn babies were placed in cribs with a special recording device that recorded the extent and direction of their head movements.[2] At the sound of a tone, if the baby turned his head to the right he received a sweet-tasting solution in his mouth. If a buzzer sounded, the baby had to turn his head to the left to receive the sweet solution. It took only a few trials for these newborns to reach a state of perfect discrimination. Whenever the tone sounded they turned to the right, and whenever the buzzer sounded they turned to the left. And they did so without any confusion.

Indeed, the newborn can do better than that. Another group of babies learned a similar discrimination, making one response to the tone and another to the buzzer. The situation was then reversed, so that the response appropriate to the tone was now appropriate to the buzzer and vice versa. In other words, they had to unlearn the first task in order to learn the second one. Babies no more than hours old were able to do this in about ten trials.

It must be obvious that the learning demonstrated in this sort of situation depends on the existence of certain abilities besides a capacity for learning. For example, the baby must be able to tell the difference between the sounds of a tone and a buzzer. He must be able to tell the difference between a head movement to the right and a head movement to the left. He must be able to make a link between tone, head movement, and sweet taste and between buzzer, head movement, and sweet taste. That is, he must be able to connect three events that are separated in time. Furthermore, in order to reverse the discrimination, the baby must be able to disconnect the events that he has related and form a completely new set of connections.

The perceptual abilities of tone-buzzer discrimination and the motor abilities of left-right movement and discrimination between left-right movement must, I feel, be built-in, as must the capacity to form the extended connections in time that are evident in this kind of learning. However, the fact that babies pick up connections between events so readily in the first few hours after birth should caution us against ready acceptance of any statement that such-and-such an ability is innate or un-learned unless we can rule out any opportunity the baby might have had to form the connections. We just cannot be certain in many cases. The newborn's ability to learn is so astonishing that it would need only the slightest exposure for any connection to be learned.

The Perceptual World of the Newborn

There is one heroic experiment which completely escapes this criticism, because the infant in question was only a few seconds old. This was a study of auditory localization, the ability to detect the source of a sound. We adults can do this quite well. We can tell whether a sound has come from the right or the left, in front of or behind us, above or below us, and so on. We locate the source of a sound so easily and automatically that there is little reason to think it might be a problem for a baby. However, the baby's problem is apparent if we consider the structure of the ear. The ear is essentially a one-dimensional sensory receptor. Sound waves striking the ear produce exactly the same pattern of disturbance regardless of the direction from which they have come. There is nothing in the sound that reaches the ear that specifies its location at all. The way we discriminate or detect the position of sound sources is by using two ears. As shown in Figure 2.1, a sound on the right will reach the right ear a few fractions of a second before it will reach the left ear. Conversely, a sound on the left will reach the left ear a few fractions

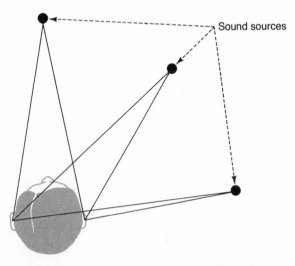

FIGURE 2.1
The more a sound source deviates from the straight-ahead position, the greater is the time difference in the arrival of the sound at each ear. When the source is straight ahead, there is no time difference. (After Bower, 1974.)

of a second before it will reach the right one. A sound coming from straight ahead reaches both ears simultaneously.

Now, this is a connection that is so automatic for adults that we are simply never aware of hearing two sounds. If a sound stimulates the right ear and then the left ear, we hear one sound on the right. But is this true for the newborn baby? Does he recognize that when a sound hits his right ear and then his left ear, he is in fact hearing one sound from his right? Or is it possible that the baby hears two sounds, both from an unspecified direction? This is a classic instance of a group of perceptual problems which may be titled problems of the *missing dimensions*. There are many dimensions of our perceptual experience that seem to have no literal correlate in the information coming into our sensory receptors. What is involved here is a translation of the sensory information we receive into the rich world we experience. The question is whether newborn babies can make this translation.

Michael Wertheimer set out to find out.[3] He gained access to a delivery room and was able to test a baby girl immediately after birth. He simply sounded a clicker on the infant's right and left and watched to see what she did. The results were surprising and fascinating. What happened was that this newborn, only seconds old, turned her eyes to the right when the sound came from the right and to the left when the sound came from the left.

Now, this indicates that the baby was able to localize the sounds in space well enough to tell right from left. However, the results also indicate something much more complex. The fact that she would turn her *eyes* toward the sound source suggests that she expected to *see* something at the source of the sound. The idea that a sound specifies something that can be seen is most surprising in the context of a newborn. It argues for some, perhaps minimal, level of *intersensory* coordination, some structure that tells the baby that the presence of information coming through one sensory modality implies the availability of information that another modality could use. This finding was completely unexpected at the time Wertheimer did his study.

A great deal of effort has been devoted to finding out how many of the missing dimensions of experience the newborn baby can supply. One area which has been studied intensively has to

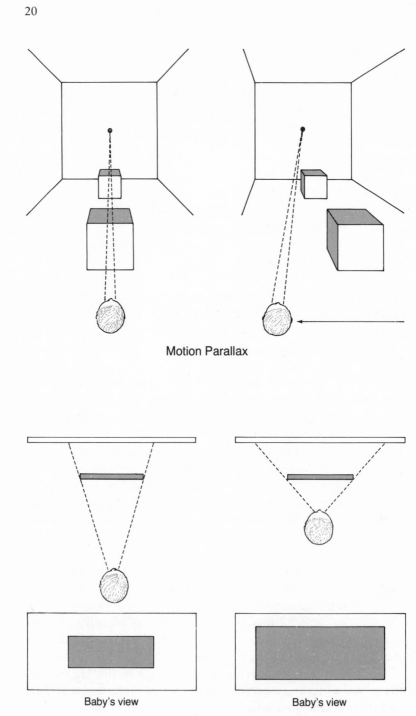

Motion Parallax

Baby's view Baby's view

Optical-Expansion Pattern

FIGURE 2.2 *(Left)*

Both these visual cues rely on movement to specify distance. Motion parallax is created by a movement of the head; a nearer object will appear to move farther and faster in the direction opposite the movement than an object that is more distant. A pattern of optical expansion is created by movement of the observer toward the object. The retinal image of an object expands with decreasing distance, and the pattern of optical expansion indicates whether the object is near or far. (Motion parallax from T. G. R. Bower, The visual world of infants. Copyright © 1966 by Scientific American, Inc. All rights reserved.)

Linear Perspective

Density Gradient

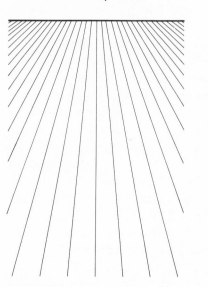

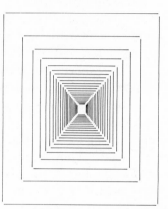

FIGURE 2.3

Monocular "painter's cues" do not require movement to specify depth and distance. Linear perspective—separation decreases with increasing distance. Density gradient—density increases with increasing distance. Other painter's cues include the interposition of objects and relative height. (From J. J. Gibson, *The perception of the visual world.* Boston: Houghton Mifflin, 1950. Used by permission.)

do with the baby's ability to perceive the third dimension of space. We adults see the world in three dimensions. We see things at different distances from us and can judge fairly accurately how far away something is. We can tell when we are moving toward something and when something is moving toward us. We make all these translations from a completely flat retinal image. There are many systems of stimulation on the retina that are correlated with the distance an object is from us. Some of these visual cues are illustrated in Figures 2.2 and 2.3.

However, none of them provides a direct representation of distance itself. They all require some translation to convert what is on the retina to what we actually see.

Again, the question is whether or not newborns can make this translation. It now appears pretty clear that they can. If we prop an infant up in a vertical position and bring an object toward his face, he will defend himself against the approaching object by pulling his head back and interposing his hands between face and object. This defensive movement has been observed in infants in the first week of life, although thus far it has not been detected in infants on the first day of life.[4]

One experiment shows that infants not only will defend themselves against an approaching object, but also can distinguish between an object approaching them on a hit path—one that appears about to strike them in the face—and an object approaching on a miss path—one that will whiz harmlessly by their heads.[5] They defend themselves against the former and not against the latter. In this experiment the approaching objects were presented as visual images on a screen (Figure 2.4). There was thus no air movement to signal an object moving toward the baby's face, as there would be with a physical object. The defensive response in this case must have been elicited by visual cues alone.

When these results first appeared, I interpreted them as an indication that newborn babies had a built-in ability to perceive three-dimensional space. A number of people took strong exception to this interpretation, pointing out that none of the infants in the study were literally newly born; all of them were several days old. I countered this objection by asking how often a baby of this age had ever been struck in the face by an approaching object. From my own observations I would have said never. However, I was reminded that the baby is quite likely to have been struck in the face by his mother's breasts during feeding. While mother and infant are still unskilled, this can, in fact, be unpleasant for the baby and could even mean potential suffocation. Babies, in fact, protect themselves in this situation with a defensive response which looks very like the defense response elicited by an approaching object.

Given the rapid learning ability of the newborn, it is altogether possible that the baby could have learned that a par-

Object on Hit Path   Object on Miss Path

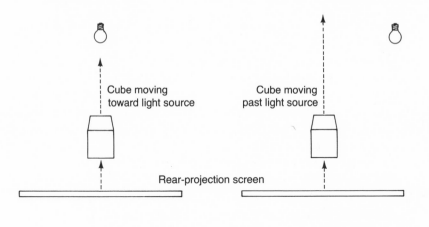

Cube moving   Cube moving
toward light source   past light source

Rear-projection screen

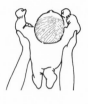   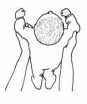

   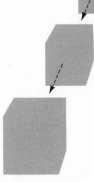

Baby's view of approaching shadow   Baby's view of approaching shadow

FIGURE 2.4

Shadows cast on a rear-projection screen were used to present babies with
optical approaching objects. Infants only a few days old were able to discriminate between an object approaching them on a direct-hit path and one approaching them on a miss path. They defended themselves against the former
and were apparently not frightened by the latter.

ticular change in the visual configuration of an object signifies a potentially unpleasant event. However, I don't think that any such objection can be made against the recent series of studies carried out by Dunkeld.[6] She found that the self-same defensive response could be elicited by a somewhat different event, perception of an object rotating so that its forward edge appeared about to strike the baby on the nose. The experimental setup is shown in Figure 2.5.

The stimulus information in this case is not the sort to which an infant would be at all likely to be exposed in the course of normal handling. Despite this, babies in the second week of life would defend themselves in this situation. As the object rotated on its axis, they moved their heads as far from it as they could, indicating that this particular change in the image signified an edge approaching their faces.

Now, this event, I would maintain, is completely unique in the world of a baby less than two weeks old. He is most unlikely to have seen a rotating object, particularly an object rotating in that plane, and is certainly unlikely indeed to have been struck in the face by such an object. Nonetheless, the babies did defend themselves. They pulled back from the approaching edge and they cried. As Figure 2.5 shows, the stimulus changes involved were subtle, and yet the babies were apparently able to integrate them, so that they saw an object rotating toward them.

These, then, are some of the perceptual abilities of a newborn baby. The newborn can localize sounds. He can locate objects visually. He seems to know that when he hears a sound, there probably will be something for him to look at, and that when an object approaches him, it probably will be hard, or tangible.* Why else would the baby defend himself against an approaching object, or the approaching edge of an object, if he didn't think it was going to be harmful? These perceptual

---

*Many people take exception to my saying that babies *know* something. Babies may show appropriate behaviors, but this does not amount to knowledge. While I would agree that babies do not know in the self-conscious way adults do, I do not believe that they are simply little machines, lacking the same kind of consciousness or awareness that we have. I think that babies can know, feel, believe, think in a way related to what adults do when they "know." In short, I think that babies are human from birth, and do not become so at some magic later date.

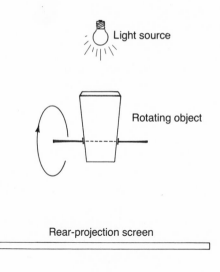

Light source

Rotating object

Rear-projection screen

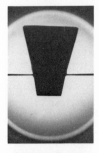

Baby's view
of rotating object

FIGURE 2.5
The shadow-casting device used to present babies with an object rotating toward the face. The photographs at the right show the sequence of shape changes the infants actually saw. (After Dunkeld and Bower, 1976a; photos by Jane Dunkeld.)

capacities would be quite unsuspected by the casual observer and could never be inferred from straightforward observation of the baby.

The Motor Abilities of the Newborn

What of motor abilities? Can a newborn baby actually do anything? Well, as we have already seen, he can move his head and his eyes to inspect the environment. He can also use these abilities in a learning experiment in order to obtain a reward. Newborns can also use their feet and their legs if they are held. A newborn (if correctly supported) will march along a tabletop or similar surface. They can also use their hands and arms to surprisingly good effect.

A young baby is normally given no opportunity to use his hands and arms. He spends much of his time on his back, and owing to the shape of his body, he will roll from side to side unless he uses his arms to maintain himself in one position. However, if a newborn is supported in such a way that his trunk is steady and his hands and arms and head are free to move, then we can observe really surprisingly efficient reaching movements (Figure 2.6). Newborn babies can reach out and hit things, and can occasionally grasp them.[7]

The newborn's reaching is not particularly accurate. Even if he is completely successful in reaching out and grasping an object, the baby doesn't seem to know what to do with it. He is most likely simply to drop it after he gets it into his hand. However, this motor skill is present and can, occasionally, be used. Because of the *latency* of the response, the time it takes to

FIGURE 2.6
A newborn baby reaching for an object. This baby is only ten days old. (Photos by T. G. R. Bower.)

organize it, under ordinary circumstances a newborn doesn't get much chance to use his grasping behavior. Potentially graspable objects just do not hang around long enough for him to reach out and take them. This may be why in most cases the behavior fades out and disappears. This is a problem we will return to later.

All the capacities mentioned so far are unexpected in newborns. None of them would be apparent to the casual eye. By the casual eye, I do not mean to exclude the scientific eye. In the course of my own research many new mothers had told me that their infants could reach out and touch things. My response was polite skepticism. I was so convinced that the textbooks were right and that reaching began at about five months—not five days—that I simply paid no attention to such reports. I was finally convinced that they had some substance when I saw my own nephew display this behavior at three weeks of age; and again when a child of a colleague who was not about to be put off by polite skepticism also did so at the age of only one week. It was only after these parents had alerted me to this behavior that I even noticed it, despite the fact that I had been working intensively with babies in this age range for several years.

In looking at infant behavior, scientists, as much as anyone else, tend to be blinded by their preconceptions about what the organism can and cannot do. They look for what they expect to see, rather than looking straightforwardly at what the organism actually does.

The Social World of the Newborn

The perceptual and motor capacities of newborn babies, surprising as they are, fade into complete insignificance when compared with their social behaviors. Just a few years ago the very idea that the newborn had social behaviors would have been greeted with total incredulity. In the course of this century, the newborn has, first of all, had to convince us that he is not a vegetable, that he requires something more than just food and water; and he has succeeded in convincing us that he is a highly intelligent animal. But it is only recently that researchers have started to gather data indicating that the newborn, in fact, thinks he is a human being and has a great many social responses directed toward other human beings.

I suspect that the newborn's social abilities are something parents could have told us about, had we ever bothered to ask them. Many parents have assumed that their babies are, from the beginning, social and make social responses. Nonetheless, there is a whole literature on processes of socialization, a literature devoted to discussing how the baby comes to be socialized, how he comes to realize that he is a human being, how he comes to have special sets of responses to people that are not elicited by anything else in his environment. A great deal of this effort, although not all of it, has, I feel, been wasted, because right from the moment of birth the baby realizes he is a human being and has specific responses elicited only by other human beings.

One of the more spectacular demonstrations of this is the fact that babies less than a week old will imitate other people.[8] If the baby's mother, or some other adult, sticks out her tongue at the baby, within a relatively short time the baby will begin to stick his tongue back out at her. (Figure 2.7). Suppose she then stops sticking her tongue out and begins to flutter her eyelashes; the baby will flutter his eyelashes back. If she then starts to open and close her mouth, for example, the baby will begin to open his mouth in synchrony. Of course, the baby will also stick out his tongue, flutter his eyelashes, and open his mouth spontaneously, but he does it to a far greater extent if there is an adult model present. Furthermore, unlike many of the other behaviors described, the newborn actually seems to enjoy engaging in this mutual imitation game.

Let us stop a second to consider the level of organization required by these behaviors. How does a newborn baby know he has a mouth? How does he know he has a tongue? And how does he know that his mouth and tongue are like the mouth and tongue he sees before him? It seems to me there must be an incredible amount of built-in intersensory mapping for the baby to be able to look at an adult sticking out her tongue and transform this information so that he knows, in this social situation, he should stick his tongue out in return. The same thing goes for any of the imitations involving the face. How many babies of

FIGURE 2.7
A six-day-old baby imitating tongue protrusion. (Photos by Jane Dunkeld.)

this age have ever seen themselves in a mirror? I think the number is very, very small. This experience does not seem to be either typical or necessary for precocious imitation to appear.

The amount of built-in intersensory coordination implied by the newborn's ability to imitate is far more astonishing than anything we have seen in straightforward studies of perceptual ability. The motor control of mouth, tongue, eyes, or fingers is more precise than anything we have seen in studies of the newborn's motor skills. And all these capacities are bent toward what is clearly, I think, a social purpose. The newborn enjoys social interaction with adults. Imitation at this stage is a social game. The responses are quite specifically directed toward human beings and seem to me to be testimony that the newborn considers himself human too. He somehow knows that his face is like the adult face he sees before him, and that his mouth is like the adult mouth he sees before him.

A point about imitation that we must bear in mind is that the activity itself seems to be very satisfying to the baby, as well as to the baby's mother. It is not an operant behavior, in the sense that babies do not imitate their mothers in order to get the mothers to do other things for them. The behavior seems to be satisfying in and of itself. The mother and the baby interact for the sake of interacting. It is for this reason that I refer to it as a social behavior. The baby doesn't have to be given food or sweet-tasting solutions or anything else to motivate him to engage in imitation. The joy that he derives from imitating seems to be unrelated to any of the more basic gratifications, such as the joy that he would get through feeding or drinking. It is something that is pleasurable and rewarding in itself.

The argument is often presented that babies come to find pleasure in human company only as a result of associating adults with food and relief from pain.[9] Imitative behavior seems to run counter to this claim. This behavior occurs spontaneously as soon as there is an adult model present. It does not seem to depend on any motivating factor connected with physiological needs and is not used to obtain any other reward. The newborn baby imitates the facial gestures of the adults around him for no reward other than the pleasure of interacting with them.

A related social behavior displayed by newborns is *interactional synchrony*. This imposing term refers to a form of behavior that is characteristic of human communication. Whenever two people from the same culture group talk to each other, a detailed analysis of their movements will show that they engage in a kind of dance with each other.[10] As one person speaks he makes certain body movements—slight posture changes, changes in head position, and so on—and the listener makes corresponding movements. People are ordinarily unaware that they are engaging in this complex dance routine, but it goes on nonetheless.

Indeed, whenever the routine is absent, there are likely to be defects or disturbances in the communication. This can be seen very clearly when two adults from different cultures try to communicate. Even when they are speaking the same language, the fact that their body language, their body movements, are quite different, may prevent them from understanding each other. The same problem occurs with some kinds of mental disturbance. In some cases the disturbed person does not engage in interactional synchrony. He may be unaware of the movements of another and may not move in any synchronic fashion himself.

With two adults, the closer the synchrony of their movements during conversation, the closer the rapport between them. In fact, the way two people move in conversation with each other can tell the experienced observer a great deal about their relationship. Daily communication depends very directly upon perhaps an unconscious awareness of these interactional, synchronic movements. Consider how much is lost in a telephone conversation in comparison with face-to-face conversation, or how much is lost in hearing only a tape recording of a conversation instead of actually seeing it on film or videotape.

All human speech is accompanied by very precise, very subtle patterns of body movement which, in fact, convey a large part of the meaning. To some extent, these patterns are culturally specific.[11] Thus individuals from different subcultures may have difficulty in communicating; each may emit signals that the other does not understand simply because, while they may communicate verbally, they do not communicate at this nonverbal, body-movement level. It is truly astonishing, therefore, to find that newborn human infants engage in interactional synchrony. When they are spoken to by an adult, they move their bodies in precise rhythms that are perfectly coordinated with the basic units of the adult's speech.

Condon and Sander conducted a remarkable study of infants about twelve hours old.[12] They presented them with tape recordings of spoken English, isolated vowel sounds, regular tapping noises, and spoken Chinese, as well as with a straightforward adult speaker. The newborns moved in precise synchrony with the peculiar structure of speech whether it was recorded or presented live. The tapping sounds produced no response, nor did the isolated vowel sounds. Although all the babies were born in the northeast United States, they all showed interactional synchrony with Chinese as well as standard American English. An instance of the complex dances the babies did is shown in Figure 2.8.

This behavior is intrinsically social; it is a distinctively social behavior. Interactional synchrony was not elicited by any of the sounds used in this experiment except human speech. This kind of communication—or communion—is obviously of great importance in a mother's feeling that her baby is responding to her. It would seem that various prenatal disturbances can reduce or abolish the baby's capacity for interactional synchrony.[13] Mothers of such babies have been known to say that their infants are simply not "cuddly," not responsive babies. This presumably means that the baby did not engage in that subtle communication routine that defines an interchange between two human beings.

There is some evidence that these failures of communication may have long-term effects on mother-infant interaction and the mother-infant relationship as a whole. A mother who feels rejected by her newborn may in turn come to reject her baby.[14] These events are rare, but they are the first instance mentioned thus far of a long-term effect of an event in infancy on later development. A baby's noncommunication with his mother in the days after birth can apparently result in prolonged noncommunication, with all the difficulties in subsequent development that this implies.

The fact that babies are social right after birth, the fact that they have a highly developed perceptual system and an astonishing ability to learn, means that we are in a position to

---

FIGURE 2.8 *(Right)*
A newborn baby moving in synchrony with an adult's words. At the first word, the left hand goes up (2). The index finger then moves across with each syllable (3, 4, 5). The right hand is raised (6), moves to the left (7, 8), and comes down again (9).

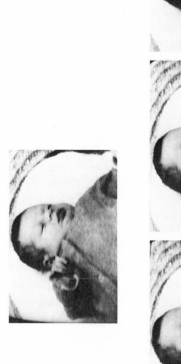

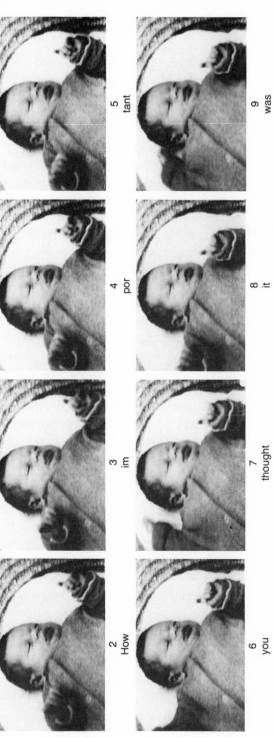

2 How

3 im

4 por

5 tant

6 you

7 thought

8 it

9 was

begin to ask the questions that so many mothers ask: Does the baby know his mother? Does he recognize me? And so on. Now, it is obvious that a newborn cannot know his own mother at birth. How soon after birth does he demonstrate that he knows his own mother? The answer, as you should expect by now, is very, very soon afterward.

In one experiment two-week-old babies were presented with their mother's face or a stranger's face, which they saw through a porthole over their cribs.[15] The mother could be silent or could be talking to her baby; the stranger could be silent or talking to the baby. The baby heard the voices through a speaker arrangement, so that the mother's face might be presented with the stranger's voice, and vice-versa. It was quite clear that the babies recognized their mothers, because they looked at their mothers much more frequently than they looked at the stranger. Furthermore, the babies seemed to know what their mothers sounded like, because there was what psychologists call *gaze aversion* whenever the faces and voices were mismatched. The infants would turn their heads away in an attempt to avoid looking at this face with the incongruous voice coming from it.

This study also produced some evidence that by the age of two weeks a baby expects his mother's face to be accompanied by her body. When the babies were shown only their mother's faces in this porthole arrangement, their behavior was somewhat strange. They would look at the face and turn away from it, then turn back and turn away again, tensing as they averted their gaze. Sometimes they turned a full 90 degrees away from the face. Carpenter, who carried out this study, concluded, reasonably enough, that the babies were surprised and disturbed to see their mother's head presented in this detached way, apparently with no body under it. They may also have been surprised to have their mothers simply stare at them, rather than talk to them or engage them in some other social interaction.

The findings on interactional synchrony in infants are a clear indication that the newborn is not a social isolate. Right from the beginning, he participates immediately and deeply in communication. The fact that babies can recognize their mothers at only two weeks shows that from the very beginning the newborn will use his extraordinary learning and perceptual abilities to serve his social needs and social wishes. In the very first days of life, babies are beginning to form social attachments. Other studies have shown that babies will protest strongly if a substitute caretaker is provided after only a few days of care by one person.[16]

A newborn thus begins life as an extremely competent social organism, an extremely competent learning organism, an extremely competent perceiving organism. In the following chapter we shall see how the newborn organizes his perceptual experiences to learn or acquire or develop more complex social behaviors.

3   The Strange Case of the Smile

The first obvious social behavior in which the baby engages is smiling. A baby's smile is considered a social response by most parents. Nonetheless, most psychologists would dispute that there is anything social in this early smile. Some define it as a reflex response to high-contrast stimuli; others attribute it to intellectual pleasure. Another possibility is that infants are actually capable of a variety of smiles, at least one of which is social.

The social behaviors of the newborn are by no means obvious. This is not the case with the baby's smile. All parents are convinced the first time they see a full-scale baby's smile that their baby is smiling at them. The full-scale smile, which emerges around the age of six weeks, is a truly wonderful response, deeply and immediately rewarding to parents and to any other recipients of it. Perhaps because of this, psychologists and pediatricians have taken great delight in trying to demonstrate that these early, wonderful smiles are not smiles at people at all, but are, in fact, responses to a variety of nonhuman events. We will describe their attempts to prove this later.

The Development of the Smile

Smiling does not appear all at once at the age of six weeks. The behavior that emerges at this point has a history. Smiles of a sort can be observed in the first few days after birth. These

FIGURE 3.1
The baby "smiling" here is only three
weeks old. (Photo by Jennifer G.
Wishart.)

early smiles usually strike the observer as false smiles. They
involve the mouth and the cheeks, but they don't seem to get as
far up as the eyes or forehead; they don't seem to have the general affective, emotional tone of the true baby smile. At this
point in life they appear spontaneously; that is to say, they will
appear while the baby is asleep, or at any rate, not awake and
not attending to stimuli from the outside world.* The smiles of a
newborn do not stir the elation that the true smile does. Most
parents put them down to gas pains or something of this sort.

By the second week of life this false smile has become more
specific, occurring most often in the presence of people, or so it
seems. The human voice, for instance, brings forth more smiles
than the sound of a bell or the banging of a rattle. In the third
week we get real smiles (Figure 3.1). They don't last as long as
the true social smiles, but they are recognizably real smiles.
They are elicited by stimulation from the outside world and no
longer seem to be spontaneous. The most effective stimulus to
elicit them is the human female voice. The visual aspects of the
speaker have no effect at this stage; even the sight of a face adds
nothing to the effect produced by a voice.

During the fifth week of life this situation changes; by the
time the baby is six weeks old, it seems that he is smiling at
human faces (Figure 3.2). In fact, a human face appears to be the
most effective of all possible stimuli for eliciting a smile from a
six-week-old baby, at this stage far outranking the voice.

---

*Small babies are not simply "awake" or "asleep." Six states of wakefulness
in small babies have been described. Only the highest state, awake and attentive
with eyes open, corresponds to what we ordinarily mean by *awake.*

FIGURE 3.2
A full-scale baby smile at six weeks.
(Photo by Jennifer G. Wishart.)

The smile response up to this point shows a genuine developmental progression.[1] In the beginning there are partial smiles; later there are complete smiles. The first complete smiles appear to be elicited by the human voice; later the controlling stimulus shifts to the human face. This is an interesting developmental progression, and one that is evidently determined entirely by the processes of growth and gene expression. This assertion can be made with some confidence, since it has been established by natural experimentation. Natural experimentation in this case is made possible by the fact that not all babies are born after the normal gestation period of forty weeks. Some are born before their *conceptual age*, their age as measured from the date of conception, has reached forty weeks; others are born later than this. A number of studies have shown that babies start to smile at human faces at the conceptual age of forty-six weeks.[2] At this point a baby's chronological age might be six weeks, it might be eighteen weeks, or it might be only two weeks, depending on his conceptual age at the time of birth. If we want to predict when a particular baby will smile at a human face, we can disregard his chronological age and consider his conceptual age. Babies smile at a conceptual age of forty-six weeks, regardless of their chronological age, regardless of how long they have actually been in the world.

The smiling that occurs at this age, seemingly directed at the human face, for long was called social smiling. It is invariably interpreted by parents as a social act: the baby is smiling at his mother, his father, his grandmother, or whomever. This naïve interpretation of the baby's smile leads us to smile back and begin to treat the baby as one of us. Although parents are elated by the smiles the baby directs toward them, for some years now psychologists have been insisting that these smiles are not social at all. They contend that when a baby smiles at a human face, he is not really smiling at the face, but at something much less human.

Smiling and Perceptual Development

A number of years ago it was discovered that there was no need to present a whole face to make a baby smile. A crude mask, a plate with two blobs on it, would elicit smiles, apparently just as well as a human face would. We might speculate that the newborn simply can't tell the difference between a face and a plate with two blobs on it, that he just doesn't notice that a plate with two blobs on it is missing a nose, hair, ears, a mouth, and so on. This idea is not really very plausible, given the perceptual abilities of the newborn described in the last chapter. A baby can perceive a tongue and a mouth well enough to imitate their movements with his own tongue and mouth. It is unlikely that he simply fails to notice that they are not there when he looks at a blobby plate. Anyway, the idea of this kind of confusion becomes even less tenable when we consider other stimuli that elicit smiles from six-week-old babies.

One of the most effective stimuli is a card with three pairs of dots on it. A card with three pairs of dots on it is more effective than a card with one pair of dots on it; indeed, it is more effective than an actual human face.[3] If the baby can tell six dots from two dots, he can surely tell two dots from a whole face, which takes care of the speculations mentioned above. Also, there is no imaginable way a baby could confuse six dots with a human face. Six dots are nothing like a face, and yet they always get more smiles than a face does. Results of this sort have led many investigators to say that the smiling we call social is not smiling at all in the adult sense. It is merely a behavior elicited by high-contrast stimuli, particularly pairs of stimuli—two black dots on a white ground, or better yet, six black dots on a white ground—with nothing specific to humans in the stimuli eliciting the response. It follows that babies smile at a human face, not because there is anything special about it, but simply because the average face contains two dark areas—the irises of the eyes—surrounded by two white areas—the sclera of the eyes—and this pair of high-contrast stimuli elicits a smile as would any pair of high-contrast stimuli.[4]

Most theorists who argue that babies smile initially only at high-contrast stimuli are faced with the problem of explaining why it is that babies come in time to smile specifically at human faces—as they do. The sort of stimulus that elicits smiles from a baby changes quite dramatically with age, as shown in Figure 3.3. Certainly by the age of four months the baby will *not* smile

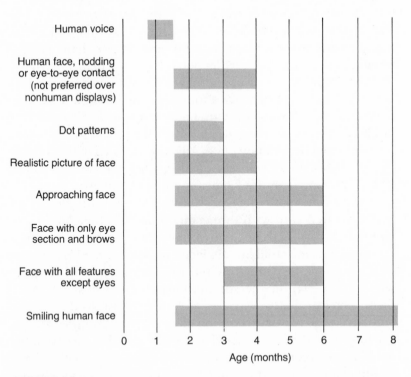

FIGURE 3.3
The stimuli that elicit smiles from babies become increasingly specific to the human face.

at six dots. A whole face, and preferably a familiar face, is necessary to make the baby smile. How is it that the baby comes to
smile specifically at faces if he starts out smiling at high-
contrast patterns? The contention is that the baby, by smiling at
the high-contrast pattern of a human face, elicits such loving
attention from his human caretakers that he comes to associate
the other characteristics of the human face with pleasure, the
pleasure he gets from the attention given him. As a result, he
begins to smile with pleasure whenever he sees a human face.
The initial smiling at high-contrast blobs, according to this
view, sums together with the pleasure that is a consequence
of this behavior to produce a smile that is specifically directed to
human beings.

This theory of the development of smiling is, in fact, quite
complicated. It assumes two causes for smiling: one, the external stimulus, a high-contrast pair of blobs; and two, an internal
stimulus, pleasure or the feeling of pleasure associated with attention from humans. Because smiling elicited by blobs produces attention from adults, which produces pleasure in the
baby, and this in turn produces more smiling, the total smile
becomes associated with all the characteristics of the adult
human face. Hence, when a baby sees a face, he smiles in part
because he sees a pair of high-contrast blobs and in part because
he expects some pleasure from his interaction with the human
adult—or so the theory goes.

Smiling and Cognitive Development

The theory outlined above certainly goes some way toward
dehumanizing the smile. However, there are other theories and
other studies which suggest that even the smile to the high-
contrast blobs is a derived or learned response, indicating that
the true cause of smiling is something more subtle and more
basic.

Many years ago it was thought that babies smiled at faces
because they associated faces with relief from the discomfort of
hunger or thirst. It was shown that this was not the case in a
somewhat bizarre study in which a pair of twin girls were

brought up without ever being given the opportunity to see an actual human face.[5] As infants, they were dressed, fed, changed, and bathed in such a way that they really didn't have a chance to associate the human face with any of the pleasurable release these activities would bring. Nonetheless, they started to smile on schedule—just like normal babies, at the conceptual age of forty-six weeks. We can come to a similar conclusion if we look at premature babies, who have had much longer experience with pleasurable relief in the context of human beings than full-term babies. They don't start to smile any earlier in terms of conceptual age than do full-term babies or even post-term babies, who have had a briefer period of experience with adult care.

It seems, therefore, that the hypothesis that early smiling is a learned response, resulting from the association of human faces with release from discomfort, is, in fact, incorrect. However, a more ingenious form of this same hypothesis has recently been advanced by J. S. Watson. Watson was not initially concerned with the causes of smiling in early infancy. He was interested in the learning abilities of young babies, the baby's detection of a contingent relationship between some particular behavior and an event in the external world.

In the experiment discussed in Chapter 2, newborn infants learned to turn their heads to the right or to the left to receive a sweet-tasting substance. There the contingency was between an action performed by the baby and the delivery of a food substance to his mouth. There have also been numerous demonstrations of learning in situations where food is not given. For example, babies will turn their heads to make an adult peek-a-boo at them, or to switch on a projector so that they have something to look at. They will kick their feet or learn to pull a string to make a mobile turn.[6] In all these cases what the baby is learning is that some behavior of his has a predictable effect on the world.

What Watson noticed was that in the process of detecting a contingency the baby smiles vigorously. These smiles seem to be caused by discovery of the contingency and to manifest the pleasure that the baby feels at having successfully detected what to do to make a particular event happen.[7] The smiling, in other words, indicates an intellectual pleasure, a pleasure at having discovered something about the causal structure of the world, and pleasure at being in control of some part of the world. At first glance, this assertion may seem to stretch credibility too far. Who would suspect that infants were susceptible to intellectual pleasure? Who would think of them as intellectual at all? Nonetheless, I think there is clear evidence that babies do derive great pleasure from problem solving, from intellectual mastery of some bit of their environment, from comprehension of some aspect of the causal structure of the world around them.

Indeed, it now seems that our unwillingness to admit that infants are capable of intellectual pleasure has been responsible for many of the difficulties we have had in demonstrating learning in infants. Newborns are quite happy to learn for a sweet taste; other babies in other experiments have been happy to learn in order to switch on a projector, make a mobile move, or make an adult jump up in a game of peek-a-boo. The Czech psychologist Papousek discovered that the actual characteristics of the event the baby was producing were quite unimportant.[8] What was important was that there be a relationship between a given behavior and a given event in the external world. Babies would indeed learn until they had figured out just what behavior of theirs produced the event. At this point there was vigorous smiling and cooing which was not directed at the event in particular, but rather seemed to reflect some internal pleasure.

Papousek also noticed that once the babies had detected the contingency, they were quite happy to stop performing in the situation, and would start again only if the contingency was changed. For example, when a baby learned that by turning his head to the right he could switch on a light, he would no longer make rightward head turns with any particular frequency. However, when the contingency was changed, so that he had to turn his head to the left to make the light come on, he would sooner or later notice that his turn to the right didn't make the light come on, and there would be a rapid burst of activity until the baby figured out what movement was necessary to switch on the light. Then, again, there would be vigorous smiling and cooing and a diminution of activity. If the problem was then made more complicated still—for example, a turn to the left and then to the right—the process would repeat itself. The baby would notice that a left turn by itself no longer had any effect. There would be a burst of activity. The baby would eventually discover the proper combination of movements, and then activity would subside.

Papousek was able to get young babies to master quite complex problems in this situation. For example, they learned to make two turns to the right, followed by two turns to the left, or a right-left, right-left combination of turns. In all cases there was a great deal of smiling whenever the baby solved the problem. After the problem had been solved, the baby no longer tried to switch the light on, so the light itself was clearly not the reason for the smiles. The conclusion is inescapable that it was the pleasure in solving the problem that produced the smiles.

Other experimenters have noticed the same thing. For example, Hunt and Uzgiris gave identical mobiles to two groups of infants in their cribs.[9] With one group of babies the mobiles were set in motion, and the babies had no control over them. With the babies in the other group, the mobiles were attached to the crib so that the babies could set them in motion by moving the crib. These babies showed clear smiling and cooing behavior while they were controlling the mobiles. Those in the other group attended to the mobiles, but did not coo or smile to any significant extent.

Watson ran a similar experiment with infants of six to eight weeks.[10] One group of babies had control over their mobiles; the others did not. Just at the point at which the babies that had control realized they had control, as evidenced by the amount of control activity they engaged in, they began to smile vigorously. As soon as they detected the contingency they began to smile.

Watson also worked in a clinical situation with a much older baby, a baby of about eight months who was developmentally arrested. The child had scarcely moved since birth and had never been seen to smile. What Watson did was give the baby a mobile which she could control with head movements, with arm movements, or with foot movements. Within two hours of exposure to this situation the baby began to move more than she had done before. Even more surprising, and in striking confirmation of Waton's hypothesis, was that in the contingency situation this baby began, for the first time, to smile. This particular baby had certainly had ample human care and consistent exposure to human faces. Nonetheless, the first smiles in her eight months of life appeared in this contingency situation. It seems that for this baby the pleasure of controlling the object, controlling some aspect of her environment, was the critical event that produced smiling.

I, myself, worked with a blind baby who, at eight weeks of age, did not smile at all.[11] The baby had been blind from birth and so, of course, had been deprived of the visual stimuli that normally elicit smiling. However, when he was given an auditory mobile and contingent control over it, so that by kicking his legs he could produce a change of sound, he began to smile and coo. The smiles were vigorous and forceful. Normally at this age we cannot elicit smiling with sounds at all, particularly mechanical sounds of the sort that we used in this experiment. Nonetheless, as soon as the baby had contingent control over this event in his external world, he began to smile. The stimulus objects in this case were small bells. Prior to the experiment the sound of these bells had not made the baby smile, and bells alone never produced a smile. Only when he was exercising control over the bells did we see smiling at this early age.

The problem is to get from smiling as a consequence of pleasure in problem solving to smiling at faces. Watson points out that in the western world the infant is most likely to be presented with contingent relationships he can detect in play situations with an adult. In fact, the games adults play with infants are all basically contingency-detection games. An adult may sit opposite a baby, and every time the baby opens his eyes wide, the adult will touch him on the nose, poke him in the tummy, blow at him, or something of this sort. Every time the baby moves his arms, the adult might make a face at him, or every time the baby kicks, the adult might say "boo." All these games present the baby with an opportunity to detect a contingency between a behavior of his own and an event in the external world.

As the baby plays these games with adults, he comes to associate the pleasures of problem solving with the presence of adults—that is, people become associated with the pleasure that is inherent in the game of contingency detection. As Watson puts it, "the contingency-detection game is not important to the infant because people play it; rather people become important to the infant because they play the game."[12]

Strange as this hypothesis may seem, it does fit with the evidence described above. It also explains some rather strange data from an earlier study. Some years ago Watson found that a face in the same orientation as the baby's face was most effective in eliciting smiling.[13] An average Western baby ordinarily sees his mother's face at a 90 degree orientation when she is feeding him, washing him, changing him, or even putting him in the bath. It is only when an adult is playing a contingency-detection game with the baby that he ever sees an adult face at exactly the same orientation as his own. Despite the greater familiarity and frequency of other orientations, it is the zero-degree orientation that is most effective in eliciting smiles. In fact, for a fourteen-week-old infant a face at zero degrees was twice as effective an elicitor of smiles as one at 90 degrees or 180 degrees.

This finding clearly casts doubt on the thesis that babies smile only at high-contrast blobs. There are high-contrast blobs in 90 degree faces, and also in 180 degree faces, but they are not as effective as those in zero-degree faces. The only plausible explanation for this, it would seem, is Watson's thesis that smiling is a response to the pleasures resulting from problem solving, and that faces are associated with these pleasures—faces in the particular orientation the adult adopts in playing games with the baby.

This, then, is the strange case of the smile, a behavior that seems unmistakably social to most parents and quite nonsocial to many psychologists. Is the response elicited by events in the external world? Is it specifically a response to people? Does it reflect intellectual pleasure, or what? One distinct possibility is that the controversy here is ill-founded. I propose that we do the infant a great disservice when we speak of "the smile" or "the smiling response." No one would think of referring to *the* smile of an adult; adults have many smiles—the scornful smile, the triumphant smile, the pleased smile, the welcoming smile, the flirtatious smile, and so on. No one has done the young baby the favor of looking at his smiles to see if they are, in fact, qualita-

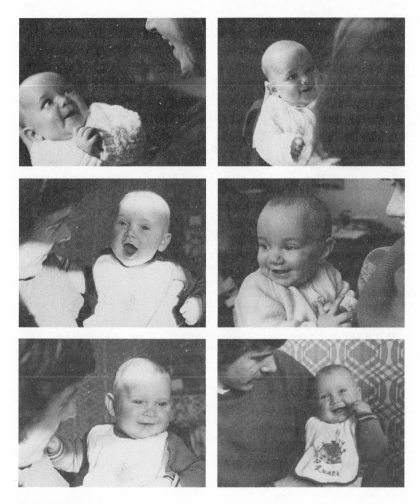

FIGURE 3.4
It is apparent that all these smiles are not the same. Does it make sense, then, to assume a single cause for all of them? (Photos by Jennifer G. Wishart.)

tively different in qualitatively different situations (Figure 3.4). Many years ago Washburn did study the smiles of older babies and found that there were numerous different kinds of smiles associated with numerous different situations.[14]

It may well be that the interpretations discussed thus far have *all* been quite correct—that babies do smile at faces in a sociable sort of way, and that babies do smile from pleasure when they manage to control a mobile. Smiling toward people is often described as coy or flirtatious in the early weeks of smiling, whereas smiling at mobiles and contingency situations has, to my knowledge, never been so described. Similarly, some of the investigators who have found that babies smile at flickering lights, or three pairs of black dots, have commented that the babies initially seemed slightly surprised. It is perfectly possible that babies thought these presentations were funny. Adults smile when they see something funny; why shouldn't babies? There is no reason why they shouldn't find the same things funny that we do.

It seems to me that the solution to this strange case of the smile is still to be found. We will have to look at the situations that elicit smiling—all the situations described in this chapter—and look more closely at the behavior. It may well be that the smiles are different in each situation, that the baby has a social smile, a smile of appeasement, a smile of triumph, and so on. We know that this is the case by the end of the first year. And it is possible that with more precise techniques, with higher-speed cameras, and the like, we could find these distinctions in embryonic form at much earlier ages. I do not think we will ever arrive at an answer so long as we insist that there is only one smile. Certainly very early in life there are a variety of smiles. These smiles have different effects on us; it is surely possible that they also have different causes.

4 The Rise of Attachments

The formation of a clear attachment between mother and infant is signaled by the appearance, at around the age of eight months, of a fear of strangers and anxiety at separation. This is supposedly because the baby has come to identify his mother as the universal provider of nurture and comfort, and her departure means the loss of these fundamental requirements. The phenomenon of child-child attachments, where nurture is not an issue, suggests another explanation. The attachment that forms between mother and infant is, in fact, a rich channel of communication—a form of nonverbal communication that is highly specific to these two human beings. Thus the approach of a stranger or the departure of the baby's mother evoke fear precisely because the baby has learned to communicate, but with only one other person.

Smiling is a pleasant social behavior. It is the most significant aspect of social development to occur in the first half-year of life. The second half-year is marked by the emergence of behaviors which are much less pleasant in affective tone. Somewhere around the age of eight months, the baby begins to manifest quite clearly a fear of strangers. At this stage, at the approach of a strange adult, the baby will cry, scream, or otherwise try to avoid the encounter. If the baby is mobile, he will try to crawl away. At a slightly later age, a baby will begin also to show fear of separation from his mother. Separation from the mother will lead to attempts to rejoin her, screaming, stillness, tears, and other signs of distress. Both these behaviors are an unmistakable sign that the baby has formed a critical social attachment.

Stranger Fear and Separation Anxiety

As with smiling, stranger fear and separation anxiety do not spring full-fledged from the baby's head at the age of eight months. During the newborn period the baby shows a distinct preference for his mother. Even at the age of two weeks, he shows some aversion when a stranger speaks to him, particularly if the stranger speaks to him in his mother's voice.[1] This behavior is certainly akin to the anxiety that we see in the eight-month-old. Similarly, in the newborn period babies become upset if they are taken care of by a stranger while their mother is away, which might be an embryonic form of separation anxiety.

Other negative behaviors toward strangers appear at various points between the newborn period and the age of eight months. Ambrose observed that babies of about fourteen weeks would simply stare at strangers, rather than smiling at them as they would at a familiar person.[2] Other investigators have reported that babies of four to five months actually "freeze" when a strange adult approaches them.[3] They will sit completely still, hardly moving a muscle, hardly breathing. This kind of freezing in nonhuman animals is taken as an index of fear, and it would seem reasonable to conclude that it indicates fear in these babies as well. None of this early behavior, however, has the intensity of the responses that can be seen in the eight-month-old (Figure 4.1). The fear of strangers, in the classic sense, gets off the ground at about this age—and gets worse. It reaches a peak during the second year, and then declines.

There is an odd interaction between fear of a strange person and fear of a strange place. A baby approached by a stranger will, under ordinary circumstances, show fear. If, however, the baby is in a strange and novel environment, particularly in the open air, he may voluntarily approach this stranger and ask to be picked up.[4] There is also an odd interaction between stranger fear and the presence of the baby's mother. A baby sitting on his mother's lap is most unlikely to show fear when approached by a stranger. A baby in a strange environment with his mother completely absent may also not show stranger fear. However, a baby whose mother is present, but not holding him, may show

FIGURE 4.1
The response of an eight-month-old baby to a stranger's attempts to communicate. (Photos by Jennifer G. Wishart.)

much greater stranger fear than in any other situation. This is an odd finding indeed.

Separation anxiety appears slightly later than stranger fear. It is typical for the baby to protest at any separation, any loss of contact with his mother or usual caretaker. If a baby is left by his mother, he will usually reject any attempt at comfort by others. In the case of a prolonged separation, the baby may fall into an apathetic state, and in the end may interact with new caretakers. When his mother comes back, he will typically cling to her very strongly, but at the same time be negative, occasionally ignoring her or pretending not to recognize her. Separation anxiety in a baby is a painful sight; it elicits a great deal of sympathy from all those who see it. It is sympathy that is pretty much pointless, for all attempts at comfort lead to naught. Indeed, they seem only to increase the baby's distress.

Separation anxiety usually refers to the anxiety a child feels when separated from his mother or customary caretaker. In fact, in an extensive study, Schaffer and Emerson found that the mother was by no means invariably the target of separation anxiety.[5] Some of the babies apparently did not care about being separated from their mothers, but protested very painfully at any separation from their fathers. Sometimes grandparents were the target. It is claimed that, in the beginning, at least, separation anxiety normally has only one target; that is to say, the child will protest at being separated from his mother, but not at being separated from his father. However, no less than one-third of the babies in this study showed anxiety at separation from two people right away. They were attached to more than one person by the time any separation anxiety appeared.

By the age of eighteen months, only 13 percent of these babies had only one target for their separation anxiety, and nearly one-third of the group protested at the departure of as many as five individuals. The standard pattern thus seemed to be that the baby develops a strong attachment to one individual, and the departure of this individual leads to separation anxiety. As the baby grows older, he forms more and more attachments, and the departure of any one of these people can lead to separation anxiety. While this pattern from single to multiple attachments is the rule, it is by no means universal. As noted above, about a third of the babies in the group studied showed multiple attachments at the outset.

Separation anxiety and stranger fear have deservedly received a great deal of attention from psychologists and pediatricians. It is almost inevitable that any child will be separated from his mother for a few hours or a few days during the course of his infancy. Thus it would seem to be in everyone's best interests to mitigate the unpleasantness of such separations. It is also usually impossible for a baby to avoid strangers in the course of a normal life.

Conventional Theories of Separation Anxiety

A variety of ingenious theories linking stranger fear and separation anxiety have been offered. Spitz suggested many years ago that a child shows fear of strangers because the sight of them reminds him that his mother is not there.[6] In other words, separation anxiety is the basic fear, and stranger fear derives from that. Certainly the absence of stranger fear when a child is on his mother's lap points in the direction of Spitz's hypothesis. However, the fact that this fear may also vanish in the total absence of the mother would seem to me to argue against this hypothesis. While it is possible that stranger fear and separation anxiety are linked—a question we will consider later—I do not think the linkage is as simple as Spitz's hypothesis implies.

What are the causes of separation anxiety? The immediate cause—the mother's departure—is obvious, but how does her departure come to cause the pathetic behavior we label separation anxiety? One broadly accepted theory is that throughout infancy absence of the mother has been associated with discomfort, just as her presence has been associated with relief from discomfort. By the processes of *associative learning*, therefore, the baby has come to anticipate discomfort whenever his mother leaves.

Despite its wide acceptance, this theory cannot account for many of the facts. Schaffer and Emerson found, for example, that about 20 percent of the babies in their study had as a target for their separation anxieties some person who took no part in their physical care whatsoever—none at all.[7] The persons in question had never relieved these babies from physical discomfort, so their departure could hardly signal incipient future discomfort. And yet they were the targets of separation anxiety. Their departure elicited just as much protest as did the departure of more conventional targets for other babies.

Schaffer suggests that the characteristic that determines whether or not a particular adult will become the object of the baby's separation anxiety is the social attentiveness of the adult to the baby.[8] In other words, it is not physical care that is important to the baby, but social attentiveness or social interaction. This observation is a strong challenge to the conventional theories of separation anxiety.

There are numerous other findings which point in the same direction. Robertson, who has done a great deal of work on ways of mitigating separation anxieties, found that the presence of a sibling, a brother or sister, is a major factor even when the sibling is a younger baby.[9] Now, while it is possible that an older child might play some nurturant role in the life of a younger one, in the age range we are talking about—babies and toddlers—it is less than likely that the younger child would ever have played any nurturant role for the older one. And yet the presence of the younger child will mitigate the separation anxieties of the older child.

Similarly, there is a great deal of evidence on twin babies, concerning both separation anxiety and the effect of separation from each other, that argues against the conventional theories. In the case of my own twin daughters, the first separation occurred when they were just under a year old. They were separated because one twin was sick and we didn't want the other one to catch the infection. Despite the presence of both parents, the healthy twin showed quite a bit of separation anxiety. She crawled from her crib and attempted to get into the room where her sick sister was. When she was taken away from that room, she cried persistently, only quieting when her sister was brought out. When they were separated again, similar vigorous protests occurred. There can be no question that these infants had ever nurtured each other. This had never happened. And yet when they were separated, we saw separation anxiety in its full, classic form.

There are numerous studies of twins in the literature which all point to the same conclusion. Twins do suffer separation anxiety, even in infancy, when separated from one another. When the object of a child's attachment is another child of the same age, we can hardly invoke fear of discomfort, fear of loss of nurture, to explain this behavior.

The most striking instance of child-child attachment is the tragic group of refugee children described by Freud and Dann.[10] Shortly after the birth of these children, their parents were deported and killed. The babies were brought together in a concentration camp when they were about six months old. There were six of them. They were looked after by a continually changing, continually overworked, continually threatened group of adults. These six were the only babies in the concentration camp. They had no stable adult attachment figures. None of the adults who looked after them, in fact, lived beyond the end of the war.

At the end of the war, the six babies were sent first to Czechoslovakia and then to England. When they arrived there they showed clear patterns of attachment behavior, but the attachments were to one another. They showed no attachment to any adult. No signs of separation anxiety appeared when they were separated from adults, but there was tremendous separation anxiety if they were separated from one another.

Now, these children had never nurtured one another. When they arrived in England as three-year-olds and were studied for the first time, they were barely old enough to do anything for one another even then. Moreover, they had been through all kinds of unimaginable horrors and stresses. According to any learning theory, they would have associated one another with stress, discomfort, and loss. They did not show this in their behavior. They were deeply attached to one another, and to no one else. A case of this sort quite clearly defies the conventional theories of nurturance as the source of all social attachments.

A Communication Theory
of Attachment Formation

In this context, I think the most appropriate starting point is Schaffer's observation that it was those adults who were socially attentive to the baby who were likely to become the targets of separation anxieties, not the adults who physically cared for them. In the concentration-camp situation, the only people likely to be attentive to the babies were the other babies.

Now, what does social interaction and social attentiveness do for the baby? Recall the examples of interactional synchrony discussed in Chapter 2. Right from the beginning of life, babies are ready to communicate in some fashion with any adult around them. Ordinarily the baby will communicate with his mother. This communication is, of course, nonverbal, but it is communication nonetheless. Over a period of time each baby and mother develop a particular, individualistic communicational style, a style of interaction specific to that mother and that baby. Trevarthen has shown that the communication routines used by a mother and her baby become more complex, more specific to them, the older the baby gets.[11] Indeed, by seven months or so, the age at which separation anxiety starts to appear, mother and baby have established quite well-worked-out routines for communicating with each other. These routines are recall, nonverbal, but are specific to mother and baby.

Now, what happens when the mother leaves the baby with someone else? The baby's only partner in communication is gone, and the baby is left with a stranger, someone who doesn't "speak the same language," who doesn't respond to the baby's social gestures, social invitations, social ploys, or other forms of interaction. The baby is, in effect, left alone. He is isolated from other adults by the very development of the communication routines he shares with his mother. As we know from the work of Schachter and others, human adults cannot tolerate solitude.[12] It seems to me very unlikely that babies can tolerate solitude either. When their mothers go off and leave them they are, for all intents and purposes, alone, completely isolated, because they have learned to communicate and interact with one specific person.

Twin babies, of course, learn to communicate with each other, probably more efficiently than they do with any adult (Figure 4.2). This is, I think, why twins characteristically show separation anxiety when separated from one another. Similarly, with respect to Robinson's observation about mitigation of separation anxiety, two children from the same family will obviously communicate with each other to some extent. Thus, even if their primary attachment figure, their mother, is gone, they are not completely alone. They still have one another, and hence someone with whom they can interact.

The newborn, remember, is ready to interact with anyone in any way. After some months with one communication figure—a communication figure who employs some particular sequence or combination of vocalization, body movement, or body contact in a given situation—the child comes to expect certain patterns of interchange and is prepared to respond appropriately. If these patterns of interchange are not forthcoming, the baby is alone. In light of William James' statement that

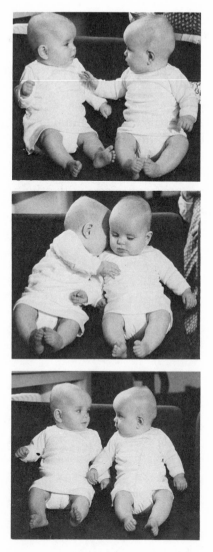

FIGURE 4.2
Seven-month-old twins communicating with each other. Twin babies
characteristically become closely attuned at an early age. (Photos by
Jennifer G. Wishart.)

the original source of terror is solitude, we can surely empathize
with these babies, communicationally isolated on the departure
of their primary communicational partner.

There is evidence that babies growing up in close proxim-
ity also learn to communicate with one another and become
communicationally attuned. Just how well depends on their

level of motor skill and their own individual temperaments. Babies of less than a year will characteristically exchange strings of vocalizations; they vastly enjoy doing this. The more closely attuned they are, the greater the loss whenever a communicational partner goes.

It follows from this viewpoint that separation anxiety should diminish when the child's mastery of communication skills reaches a level at which he can communicate with anyone. This, in fact, seems to be the case. Separation anxiety declines once the child starts to talk—and declines step by step with his mastery of language and his ability to communicate with others in his environment. It would be possible to interpret the pattern of decline in Figure 4.3 in other ways. The most compelling

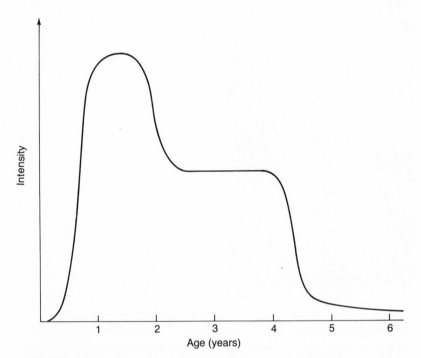

FIGURE 4.3
The changes in intensity of separation anxiety with age. The data are compiled from a number of studies; hence the curve is only a general indicator of the direction and rate of change in the response.

explanation, however, is that the ability to communicate is responsible for the decline in separation anxiety, just as the inability to communicate in a world of strangers is responsible for its rise.

This analysis of separation anxiety also illuminates the question of stranger fear. For an eight-month-old baby, a stranger is someone with whom he cannot communicate, someone with whom he has never tried to communicate. In fact, we are likely to see stranger fear only when a stranger tries to interact with the baby.[13] As long as the stranger ignores the baby, the baby will usually show no particular aversion. If the stranger makes an overt attempt to communicate with the baby, however, the result is likely to be stranger fear in its fullest form. From the baby's standpoint, he is being approached by someone much larger than he is, who is addressing him in a foreign tongue, obviously expecting to be understood. It is not surprising that such a situation is fear provoking.

Wahler conducted an experiment with three-month-old babies in which a stranger provided the babies with social reinforcement for smiling.[14] What he found was that the babies smiled at the stranger more before the stranger tried to interact with them than they did either during or after these attempts. I think this shows that the stranger was simply not using the communication routines that each of these babies was accustomed to. Hence, instead of being a source of pleasure, the stranger's overtures were simply a source of puzzlement. The babies were only puzzled, rather than fearful, because at three months they had not yet developed the highly specific patterns of interaction necessary to attach them firmly to their own communicational partners.

In other words, stranger fear and separation anxiety are a natural consequence of the baby's ability to learn—in this case, to learn specific communication skills. As these skills become more refined, they effectively isolate him from everyone who doesn't share that particular communicational code. This means that the baby must, of necessity, develop a certain level of communicational ability in order to form the kind of attachment evidenced by stranger fear and separation anxiety.

This viewpoint is in contrast to the argument derived from ethology, that there is a critical period for attachment formation, as in *imprinting*, a process studied mostly in birds. Apparently, if newly hatched birds fail to form an attachment by a specific age, they never will be able to do so. In other words, in the case of imprinting there is a critical period for development. Some people have concluded from the findings on birds that there may also be a critical period in human infants for the formation of attachments. This doesn't seem to be the case. Rather, the ability to learn seems to be what is critical.

This is shown, I think, quite clearly in a study of two groups of babies who had been hospitalized at an early age, before the point at which they would show such behaviors as separation anxiety or stranger fear.[15] The objective of the study was to determine how long it took the babies after they returned home to form normal attachments, as indicated by the emergence of stranger fear and separation anxiety.

One group of babies had been hospitalized in a standard institution, which had a fairly low staff-to-baby ratio. Thus the infants in this group had very little opportunity to interact with anyone. The other institution had a fairly high staff-to-baby ratio. This staff changed continually, so that the babies were rarely exposed to any one individual for more than a few hours in total. However, the staff ratio was high enough that a considerable amount of time was spent in social interaction. In social interaction with a variety of different people, the baby would have an opportunity to develop some communication skills, but not the highly specific patterns that would lead to separation anxiety and stranger fear. The babies in the institution with little opportunity for social interaction with anyone would hardly be expected to develop a high degree of communication skill. In fact, we would hardly expect them to develop any communication skills at all.

After the babies went back home, the two groups were compared to see how long it took them to develop normal attachments. The babies who had been in the poorer institution took about twice as long to become afraid of strangers. This is just what we would expect if stranger fear and separation anxiety reflect the acquisition of communication skills. The babies who had ample opportunity to develop basic communicational abilities, but not sufficient to limit them to a single partner, were able to capitalize on the skills they already had. Thus it took them only half as long to reach the level of specificity in communication that cut them off from strangers as it did the babies who had to start almost from scratch when they went home.

On the surface it might seem that the best way to avoid stranger fear and separation anxiety would be simply to avoid strangers and separations. This is not at all what is implied. The level of stranger fear can be reduced, of course, by avoiding direct attempts to interact that provoke the kind of communicational breakdown illustrated in Figure 4.1. For the most part, however, stranger fear and separation anxiety are necessary outcomes of the process of learning how to communicate, and human beings must obviously learn how to communicate clearly in order to survive in the world. The most important point, however, is that communication skills are *learned*, and while it may become more difficult for a baby to acquire this learning as he gets older, he still can do it. There is no need to invoke critical periods when we are discussing a learning process of this sort.

This brings us to the verge of a discussion of the harmful effects of separation or loss of a mother or a mother figure in infancy. Detailed discussion of this matter is postponed until Chapter 9, where we will consider the long-term consequences of experiences in infancy.

Social Interactions

Most studies of social development in infancy have focused on mother-infant interaction. Mother-infant interaction is undoubtedly the most important variable. However, we should not overlook the fact that children will interact with one another if given the opportunity to do so. There are many accounts of one-year-olds or toddlers treating one another as objects and even doing one another serious physical damage. I think this sort of behavior occurs only in children who have been isolated from other children. Twins interact very vigorously with one another by about the age of five months, as do babies in institutions. Babies in institutions will typically begin to notice other babies—the child in the next crib, for example—around the age of six months. They will signal to one another, wave, coo, babble, and so on; they apparently derive a great deal of pleasure from this.

The kind of social interaction that we can see in one-year-olds, of course, depends on a long history of prior communications between the babies in question. Two one-year-olds who have never seen another baby are indeed quite likely to do one another damage, but this is simply a consequence of their lack of familiarity with other children. It is a consequence of the fact that they have no developed routines for communicating together. Many of the problems that arise in nursery schools and kindergartens might well be avoided if babies were raised more communally, with more exposure to other babies of the same age (Figure 4.4).

If most studies have concentrated on the mother-infant relationship, it is also true that most of the attention has gone to the infant. It has been assumed that mothers respond automatically to their babies, and that it is only the baby's responses that are acquired. There is a great deal of evidence, however,

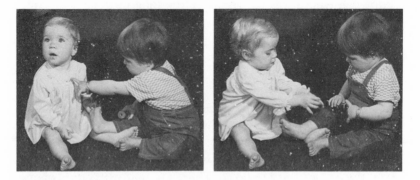

FIGURE 4.4
These ten-month-old babies were strangers to each other before this meeting. One baby pokes the other to get her attention. The second baby then asks for the toy. (Photos by Jennifer G. Wishart.)

that this is not the case. First of all, if mothers are strangers to their babies, the baby is an equally puzzling stranger to his mother, at least immediately after birth. The mother must learn to communicate with the baby, just as the baby must learn to communicate with the mother. The learning in this case is a two-way process, but a process obviously greatly affected by the preconceptions the mother brings to the situation.

In my own work I have noticed that mothers who had an initially low opinion of an infant's capacities changed these opinions when they saw their babies perform in laboratory situations, and this in turn changed the way they acted toward the baby. This kind of change seems to be quite widespread, although it is hard to quantify. There is also a great deal of evidence in the clinical literature that the expectations of a mother or a father toward their baby affects how they will interact with the baby.[16] This is particularly true of babies handicapped in some way. If the parents overestimate the handicap, their motivation for interaction may be lessened accordingly. There is an unfortunate vicious circle involved here. The handicapped baby probably needs more than the normal amount of social attention. Because he is handicapped, he will receive a less than normal quota, which may well magnify the effects of the handicap, reducing the attention given him yet further, and so on. Some evidence that the baby is not as handicapped as the parents thought, however, can again quite dramatically change the quality and quantity of the interaction.

Personality Differences

Thus far "the baby" has been referred to as if all babies were the same in their responses in social situations. This is an oversimplification. There are individual differences between any two babies placed in the same-seeming situation. Babies differ in personality just as adults do, although the differences and number of ways of differing are much fewer. Differences in personality or temperament have been detected in babies only a few hours old.[17] Quite consistent and quite large differences can be observed by the end of the first year. These differences affect the way in which the baby behaves in social situations with his mother, with strangers, and so on.

It seems probable that the differences in infant personality that appear by the end of the first year are themselves a function of the treatment a baby gets from the adults who look after him. The clearest evidence of this comes from a study of personality development in identical twins.[18] Identical twins are genetically identical. Any differences in their personalities must therefore be due to differences in the way they are treated. All the twins in this study were pairs reared together. Nonetheless, there were personality differences between them, and the amount of difference varied with the amount of difference in their appearance. Identical twins who look similar are as genetically identical as twins who look identical. However, it is virtually impossible to behave differently with twin babies who look exactly the same, whereas it is possible to do so with twins who look different. From this study it seems clear that such differences in treatment produce manifestly different personalities.

There are other aspects of personality which develop during infancy that also seem to be environmentally determined. The most surprising instance of this, to me, anyway, is the extent to which this is true of sex identity. By the age of one year boys are very different in personality from girls. Goldberg and Lewis, in comparing one-year-old boys and girls, described the boys as more independent, more interested in exploration, liking toys that require gross motor activity, and preferring vigorous play with much banging and running about.[19] Boys will be boys, in other words, by the age of one year.

The most striking evidence of the critical role of parents in producing these differences comes from studies of individuals whose biological sex differs from their labeled gender. Money has studied a number of such cases.[20] As a result of some developmental aberration prior to birth or surgical intervention after birth, it can happen that a baby who is genetically a boy will look like and be treated as a girl. The converse can happen as well. These mislabeled individuals develop in accordance with the gender assigned by their parents. If the parents think they have a girl, the child develops into a girl, and if they think they have a boy, the child develops into a boy, with all the interests and behavioral traits characteristic of boys. The genes seem powerless to redirect the sex labels given by parents.

Since these labels are effective before the end of the first year, verbal labeling is obviously not a factor. Goldberg and Lewis speculate that parents subtly reinforce the kinds of behavior they see as appropriate to the gender of their child (Figure 4.5). While these subtle processes have not been analyzed in any detail, it is clear that parents do treat boy babies and girl babies quite differently. The differences range from clothing, which can be important as a constraint on some kinds of behavior to actual social interactions. Fathers spend more than twice as much time talking to daughters as to sons; the boys are much more likely to be picked up and bounced around in rough-and-tumble play. Although the more subtle variations in

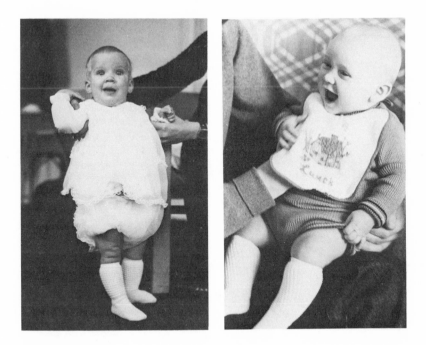

FIGURE 4.5
From infancy boys and girls are dressed, treated, and expected to behave in quite different ways. (Photos by Jane Dunkeld.)

parental behavior have not yet been delineated, there is little doubt of their presence.

In the case of the personality characteristics described thus far it would seem that it is the daily social environment of the child that determines the way the baby will behave. The individual differences between babies in standard social situations are thus, in all likelihood, a function of the individual social environments the babies live in every day of their lives.

5 Perceptual Development

The newborn has a startlingly well-organized perceptual system. Nonetheless, this system undergoes considerable development during the months after birth. The principal change is in the amount of perceptual information the baby can process, as evidenced by an increasing differentiation of sensory inputs, the baby's perception of objects, and changes in sensory-motor coordination. These developments are in part the result of greater familiarity with objects and events in the world and in part the result of growth. It is apparent from studies of blind babies that perceptual development involves an interaction of both these processes. Although growth takes place under genetic control, its direction–even with respect to the differentiation of neurological structures–depends on the information provided by inputs from the environment.

Like most other newborn primates, the human infant is ready to pick up information from the world around him as soon as he has access to it. In the months after birth, however, there is a great increase in the baby's capacity to pick up information, both in terms of absolute quantity and in terms of more differentiated information about the world. This increase in information-handling capacity is accompanied by an increasing ability to select just what information will be picked up. Both these process are illustrated by the development of *intersensory differentiation*, the ability to differentiate between inputs to the sensory structures.

Intersensory Differentiation

As we saw in Chapter 2, the newborn exhibits a certain measure of intersensory coordination in responding to stimulation from the environment. When presented with a sound, he will turn his eyes to look at the place the sound came from. When touched, his eyes will go to the place where the touch was applied. If he is shown something and given an opportunity touch it, the baby expects that there will be something there to touch, and is very surprised if there is not. This expectation is still readily apparent in much older babies in such common situations as that shown in Figure 5.1.

There is some evidence that this early coordination between the senses involves some lack of *differentiation* between one sense and another. It seems that a very young baby may not know whether he is hearing something or seeing something. For example, suppose a three-week-old baby is shown a pair of alternately flashing lights. Now, babies lose interest in this kind of repetitive event quite quickly. However, we can regain their

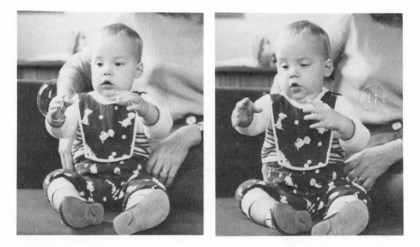

FIGURE 5.1
This baby obviously expected the three-dimensional object he saw to be tangible. (Photos by Jennifer G. Wishart.)

interest if we change the event—say, by moving the lights so that they are no longer on the baby's right and left, but above him and below him.

Suppose instead of changing the position of the lights, we change the modality of the stimulus, so that the baby hears two clicking sounds alternating in the same place he had seen the two lights. This change does not recapture the interest of a young baby as effectively as a change in the position of the stimulus. It is almost as if the very young baby knows that something is going on in these two places in space, but doesn't really notice whether the event arrives in his mind through his ears or through his eyes.[1]

This lack of sensory differentiation is found only in the youngest babies. Very rapidly, it seems, babies develop the ability to register not only the place, but also the modality of an input. Their perception thus becomes more differentiated, so that they register more information about events in the world.

The changes that occur in intersensory coordination produce interesting changes in motor behavior as well. With young babies, it seems that something that can be seen is necessarily something that can be grasped. When a young baby is presented with a *virtual object*—an illusory and intangible three-dimensional image projected in space—he grasps compulsively on the object he sees, finishing up with clenched hands every time. An older baby, by contrast, does not clench his hand on the image. He will bring his hand to its location, but will then stop, withdraw his hand, and inspect the object as a peculiar visual display.[2] Visibility and graspability are not necessarily linked for older babies, as they are for younger babies.

Similar dissociations occur with hearing. For young babies a sound specifies something that can be seen and touched. Later in development it specifies only something to be listened to. This produces a paradoxical decline in the behavior of reaching out for something that can be heard but not seen, such as a bell being sounded in the dark.[3] Babies up to about six months will readily reach toward the sound; babies older than this will not do so at all. The reasons for this change are complex, as we shall see in the next chapter.

Changes in
Information-Processing Capacity

There are parallel changes in functioning that permit the registration of more and different information. The change in the baby's response to an approaching object exemplifies this very well. As we saw in Chapter 2, newborn babies will defend themselves against an approaching object. However, if the speed of approach is great enough, there is no response at all. At a high approach speed it seems that the information is coming in too fast for the newborn to pick it up.[4] The same thing occurs with lateral movement. When an object moves across a baby's field of vision, the baby tends to track in that direction. As the crossing speed increases, the probability of tracking decreases accordingly. This is also true of adults, but the speed required is much higher. It seems quite likely that growth within the visual system accounts for these changes. Every functional part of the visual system grows, and the greater number of neural units available for vision undoubtedly permits an increase in the amount of visual information that can be processed.

Some of the changes described above may actually be changes in memory capacity, rather than perceptual ability. This is because many of the methods used to examine perception rely to some extent on memory. In one typical experiment four-week-old babies were shown an object in a lighted window.[5] The lights in the window were then switched out and, after an interval, switched on again, revealing either the original object, a completely different object, or nothing. As long as something reappeared, the babies were quite happy. It didn't seem to matter that the object was a different size, shape, and color from the one that had been visible before the lights went out. Only if the lights went on to reveal nothing did the babies act surprised.

Now, this result could mean that the babies simply hadn't noticed or perceived the size, shape, and color of the original object. Alternatively, it could mean that they had simply forgotten the size, shape, and color of this object. It seems more likely that memory is what is involved, because the results varied with the length of time the lights were out. If the dark interval was very short, then the babies showed surprise at any change in the appearance of the object.

It seems likely that memory rather than perception is also involved in some of the other changes that have been observed in the course of infancy. Consider one of the classic problems in perceptual development, the problem of shape constancy. The shape that an object projects onto the retina changes drastically with the angle at which the object is viewed (Figure 5.2). Despite

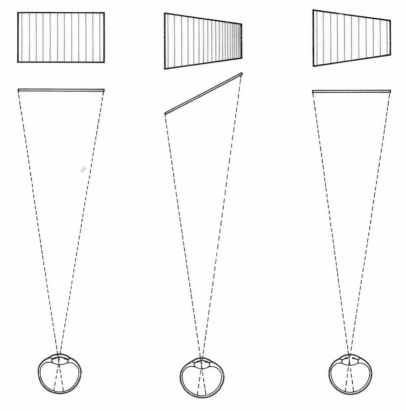

FIGURE 5.2
Shape constancy is illustrated by recognition of a shape in different orientations. A rectangle presented across the line of sight projects a rectangular image on the retina. Presented at a slant, it projects a trapezoidal image. Nevertheless, it is usually seen as a rectangle despite the fact that a trapezoid across the line of sight projects the same shape (*right*). (From T. G. R. Bower, The visual world of infants. Copyright © 1966 by Scientific American, Inc. All rights reserved.)

this, we can identify the shape of the object from any position and correctly recognize that a particular shape is the same when seen from different positions. It is widely agreed that we do this by combining the information in the retinal image with information about the orientation of the object whose shape we are computing. It seems that babies recognize shape as constant, but at first glance they appear to do so without picking up orientation information.

Consider this experiment conducted with babies of eight to twenty weeks.[6] The baby is shown a standard shape, such as a cube, for 30 seconds; the lights go out for a few seconds, and then he is shown the same shape for another 30 seconds. When this process is continued, the baby *habituates* to the cube, so that with successive presentations he looks at it less and less. If, instead of the same shape every time, the baby is shown a different shape on each presentation, then habituation does not occur.

Suppose now that we present an intermediate situation. Suppose we show the baby a cube on every presentation, but show it each time in a different orientation (Figure 5.3). If the baby perceives shape as constant, he should recognize the object

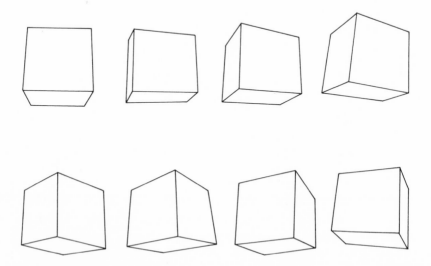

FIGURE 5.3
This figure shows the same cube in eight different orientations as presented to the babies in the experiment described in the text.

as a cube on every presentation, and so should habituate to it. However, the changes in orientation should keep up some interest if the baby notices them, so that the decline in attention should be less drastic than with the cube in the same orientation. What does happen is most surprising. The decline in attention to the cube is exactly the same whether the cube is in the same orientation or different orientations. In other words, it appears that the babies recognize the shape as constant without orientation information.

If this were actually the case, it would be a remarkable feat, for no one has been able to propose a mechanism by which the shape of an object can be recognized without taking orientation information into account. It seems much more likely that the baby picks up the orientation information in perception but simply does not put it into memory. What he remembers between presentations, while the lights are out, is that there is a cube in that window; the information about its orientation is simply not retained.

Newborns certainly can pick up orientation information, as evidenced by their response to a rotating object. However, they apparently use this information to compute shape and then throw it away. This point came out in a discrimination experiment, in which an attempt was made to teach eight-week-old babies to discriminate between a rectangle held straight in front of them and the same rectangle held at an angle to their line of vision.[7] The babies simply could not make this discrimination. The shape of the object swamped the orientation information. They made the discrimination easily however, when the shape information was taken out of the situation, as shown in Figure 5.4. With the edges of the object no longer visible, so that shape was not discernible, the babies had no trouble discriminating between the two orientations.

At this point we must draw a distinction between the baby's ability to perceive things and his ability to attend to all the things he can perceive. There is a tremendous change in attentional capacity in the course of infancy. This is probably due in part to growth of the brain, just as growth and development of the eye are responsible for changes in the amount of information the visual system can handle. However, a large part of this change is the result of ordinary exposure to objects and

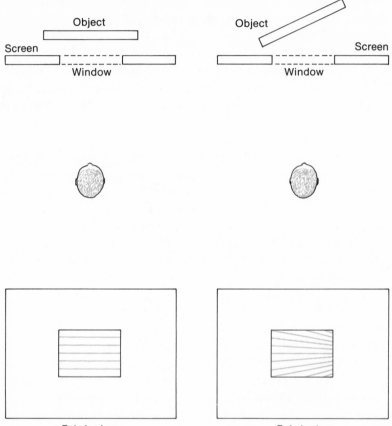

FIGURE 5.4
Although young babies do not usually discriminate orientation, apparently they are able to do so. When a striped rectangle is viewed through a window small enough to hide the shape of the object, eight-week-old babies will differentiate between the two orientations shown. (After Bower, 1966.)

events in the world. It seems that the more familiar an object is, the less attention is required to cope with it. Both these factors, the increase in attentional capacity and the decrease in the attention required by a familiar object, show up quite naturally in the course of the development of reaching. This topic properly belongs in the next chapter. However, we can discuss this bit of it here.

Young babies will reach out and bat at objects in their visual field, occasionally grasping them, usually just knocking them about. At some point in his development the baby catches sight of his hand as it enters the visual field. The sight of this hand is so riveting that the reach is stopped, and the baby's attention switches over completely to the hand. The baby may glance back at the object and begin to reach for it again, but the sight of the hand in motion will distract him, interrupting the reach yet again. This process can go on for a while, with the hand and the object competing for the baby's attention (Figure 5.5). After this point the baby focuses on his hand quite compul-

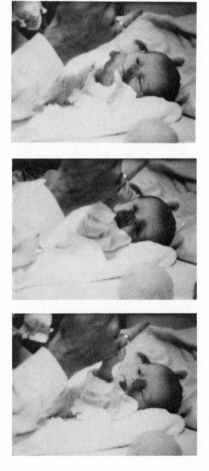

FIGURE 5.5
This twelve-day-old infant, when given a finger to reach for, looks at her hand when it comes into the visual field. As she looks back at the finger, she raises her hand to it, but the reach stops as she catches sight of her own hand again. (Photos by T. G. R. Bower.)

sively for a few days. Gradually he habituates to it and begins to reach out again without being distracted.

What seems to happen here is that the baby is initially focusing so intently on the object he is trying to reach that he doesn't even notice his hand swinging over to get at the object. With growth, his capacity for attention increases, so that he notices his hand, and this diverts attention from the object. After sufficient inspection, the hand becomes something that can be noticed without taking up much of the baby's attention. Reaching can thus operate at a much more efficient level, because the baby can now attend to the position of the object and the position of his hand simultaneously. He can thus use visual control to bring his hand to an object, a procedure that makes reaching much more accurate.

Before the hand-regard episode, the baby simply throws his hand toward an object. He does not have the attentional capacity to monitor the accuracy of his reach. If he misses the object, he will retract his hand and try again. Once he has familiarized himself with his hand, he can monitor hand and object together, enabling him to correct his reach while it is occurring.

These changes can be seen in the normal course of reaching. They are brought out more dramatically in experimental situations in which babies are fitted with wedge prisms.[8] A wedge prism displaces the input to the eye as shown in Figure 5.6. When a young baby reaches out to the place where the object seems to be, he pulls his hand back and then reaches out to the wrong place again, over and over, protesting all the while, but seemingly unable to correct for the perceptual illusion. At the start of his reaches, an older baby will aim at the wrong place, just like the younger baby. However, as soon as his hand gets into the visual field, the aim is corrected and the hand homes in on the object. This is, surely, clear evidence that older babies can attend to hand and object simultaneously, a clear tribute to their growing attentional capacity.

Further evidence of changes in attentional capacity can be found in even more artificial experimental situations. There is some evidence from learning experiments that babies simply cannot attend to all the aspects of the stimulus presented to

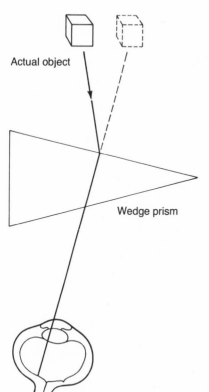

Actual object

Wedge prism

FIGURE 5.6
A wedge prism displaces the apparent
position of objects.

them. In one such experiment babies were shown the pattern in
Figure 5.7 and were rewarded for responding to that pattern.[9]
The response was a head turn and the reward was a peek-a-boo.
After the response was well established, the babies were shown
one or another of the bits of which the original pattern was
made. Babies older than twelve weeks simply did not respond to
these bits at all. Younger babies, by contrast, responded just as
briskly to the bits as to the whole pattern.

How does this show a change in attentional capacity? The
original pattern is a complex that can easily be decomposed into
the bits shown in Figure 5.7. It seems quite plausible that the
young babies in the experiment were unable to attend to all the
bits at once, so that, when presented with the whole pattern,
they attended to only one bit of it at a time. As far as they were
concerned, the whole pattern at any time consisted of one or

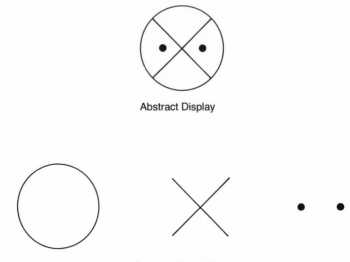

Abstract Display

Separate Test Stimuli

FIGURE 5.7
Infants who have learned to recognize this pattern will also respond to any of its components presented separately. Not until the age of about four months do they seem to notice that the rest of the pattern is missing.

another of its bits. They did not have enough attentional capacity to tell the difference between a bit of the whole and the whole. The older babies, by contrast, could attend to more than one bit of the whole, and so were instantly able to recognize that a single bit was different from the whole pattern.

Similar processes may underlie changes in that strange behavior, the smile. As we saw in Chapter 3, babies do smile at faces, for whatever reason. However, a whole face is not really important until the age of three or four months, just as in the experiment described above. It seems that young babies concentrate so much on the most significant part of the face that they do not have enough attentional capacity left over to notice the absence of the other parts. The gradual growth of attentional capacity is thus revealed in the gradual increase in the number of bits of a face necessary to elicit a smile (Figure 5.8).

In this context, too, we can see the interaction between growth and experience. Institutional infants, who have less experience of faces than do infants at home, take longer to develop their attentional capacity for faces than do home-reared babies.

Simple dots or angles.	 ● ∨	Under 6 weeks
Eye section alone; under portion of face unnecessary.		10 weeks
Eye section still suffices, but under half of face must be present even though mouth movements only fleetingly noticed; motion facilitates.		12 weeks
Eye section still suffices, with wide individual differences. Mouth gradually noticed, its movements particularly effective. Wide mouth best. Plastic model of adult effective.		20 weeks
Effectiveness of eyes lessens; mouth movements generally necessary, especially widely drawn mouth. Still no differentiation of individual faces.		24 weeks
Attention to face as such lessens; recognition of facial expression begins, with interest in other children. Progressive differentiation of individual faces.		30 weeks

FIGURE 5.8
The stimuli necessary to elicit a smile at various ages.

There is another seeming paradox in the perceptual development of infants that may be explained by the increase in information-handling capacity. As we saw earlier, infants in the newborn phase will defend themselves against an approaching object. However, it is not until the age of eight months, at least, that babies will show this defensive response if they themselves are moved toward a wall. The probable explanation of this asynchrony is that recognition of an approaching object requires attention only to the object. Awareness of self-movement, by contrast, requires attention to everything in the visual field, a feat that is surely much more difficult.

Growth of the Sense Organs

The growth of attentional capacity is perhaps the most obvious and most important aspect of perceptual development in infancy. Less obvious, but also important, are the adjustments the baby must make to the growth of his own perceptual system. We have posited growth as something beneficial to the baby. It certainly is. But growth does produce problems for the baby as well.

Consider how changes in head size affect the problem of locating sounds. We know that a sound is coming from the right because the sound waves from it reach the right ear before they reach the left ear. The farther to the right the source is, the greater the time discrepancy between the two sounds. However, the growth of the baby's head pushes the ears farther and farther apart. This means that at different points in development, the same right-left discrepancy will have different meanings (Figure 5.9). The problem for the baby is learning and then unlearning

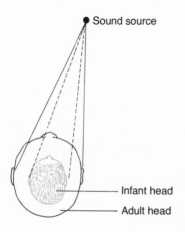

FIGURE 5.9
Because of the difference in head size, there is less difference in the arrival time of sound waves at the two ears for an infant than for an adult. (After Bower, 1974.)

the meanings of the particular discrepancies produced by his head size at the moment.

It seems that this process takes quite a long time. In one experiment, babies of various ages were seated in a dark room, with noise-making objects placed in various locations around them.[10] An infrared television camera was used to record the accuracy of the babies' reaching for the noise-making objects in each position. A control group of babies, matched for age, were shown a visible, but silent, toy in various positions. The lights were then switched out, so that the babies had to reach in darkness for the toy they had seen. Thus for the first group of babies success in obtaining the noise-making toy in darkness was entirely dependent on accurate auditory localization, which in turn depends on correct interpretation of the right-left discrepancy in sound arrival time at the two ears. For the second group success depended on some visual trace of the silent object they had previously seen in a particular position.

The accuracy of reaching to the midline, the point at which there is no discrepancy, and therefore no change with growth, was very high in the auditory case, higher even than in the visual-trace case. However, not until the age of six months was reaching to the side, where the problem is compounded by growth, as accurate for auditory location as in the case of location by visual trace.

Growth poses similar problems with visual perception. The most obvious example is in binocular vision, as illustrated in Figure 5.10. However, there are others. Consider the problem of size judgment. An object projects an image on the retina, and we use the size of that image, along with distance information, to compute the size of the object we see. Now consider the baby's problem. His eye is much smaller than the adult eye, and the retina, the sensitive surface, is not so far away from the optical system of the eye (Figure 5.11). This means that an object of a given size at a given distance will produce a much smaller image in a baby's eye than it does in an adult's eye. Furthermore, the size of that image will change during growth.

The changes in size of the retinal image will not make any difference in comparing the size of one object with the size of another. It will make a difference, however, in the judgment of absolute size, as reflected in accurate motor responses. Consider

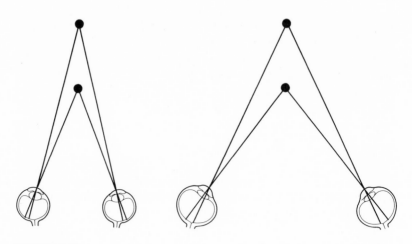

FIGURE 5.10
For objects the same distance away, the convergence angle and disparity are smaller for infant eyes than for adult eyes. (After Bower, 1974.)

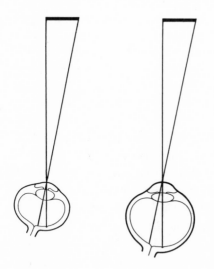

FIGURE 5.11
The infant eye is much shallower than the adult eye, so that objects of the same size will project a larger retinal image to the adult eye than to the infant eye. (After Bower, 1974.)

the problem of reaching out and grasping an object. Anyone who does this must judge the size of the object and transfer this judgment to control of his hand or hands. The changes in the size of the eye—and the far greater changes in the size of the hand—make this a terribly difficult developmental problem. Nevertheless, it is a problem that babies solve at a functional level quite early in development (Figure 5.12).

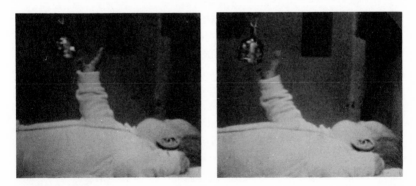

FIGURE 5.12
This baby, shown adjusting his hand to the size of the object, is less than three weeks old. (Photos by T. G. R. Bower.)

Hand regard is probably the important mediating behavior in this context. Babies can be seen comparing their hand size with object size in reaching contexts. This behavior cannot occur at too early an age because of the attentional capacity it demands. Another factor is sheer familiarity with objects. There have been observations of blind babies making successful adjustments of their hands to grasp a familiar object.[11]

There is a great deal more in development that involves the perceptual system. Much of it involves changes in the use of the perceptual system, rather than changes in the system itself. Whether this is called perceptual development or cognitive development is more a matter of taste than substance. At any rate, we shall deal with these problems in Chapter 7, keeping changes in use separate from changes in structure.

Effects of Restriction on the Perceptual System

So far we have looked at changes that are undoubtedly for the better. Unfortunately, infancy is also a period in which the perceptual system can change for the worse. Restrictions on visual experience can produce permanent alterations in the structure of the nervous system, with the result that visual inputs can never be used. The most tragic cases of this sort are babies born with cataracts. Cataract is a disease in which the lens of the eye is cloudy and relatively opaque to light. The visual experience of these infants must be akin to our experience in trying to see through a frosted-glass window. Cataracts can be treated surgically. It is possible to remove the damaged lens and fit the baby with a contact lens, so that perfectly clear images are produced on the retina. Unfortunately, it seems that if the operation is done much after the age of six months, the baby cannot make much use of these clear images. This is not just a lack of development; the baby does not even have the visual capacities of the typical newborn. By this time, considerable degeneration, or loss, has also taken place.

Loss of vision during the first six months of life has permanent effects on the ability to use vision. The loss of six months' worth of vision has progressively less effect the older the child is when temporary blinding occurs. However, the effects can still be severe as late as the age of two-and-a-half. In the classic cases cited by the surgeon Uhthoff, the children were described as having forgotten how to use vision:

> On being called to come, the child at first stands still; only when bidden more firmly does she begin to grope slowly forward, obviously directing herself by ear alone, though her eyes are wide open. Her line of advance is generally a wrong one, and she bumps into every obstacle.

And later:

> If a piece of sugar, which the child has a liking for, is thrown on the floor in front of her, so that she hears where it falls, she still does not look down at all, but gazes aimlessly straight ahead.[12]

This drastic effect on behavior resulted from only six months' loss of vision. The surgeon described his patients as "forgetting how to see." Children of this age, however, can recover the use of their sight, can remember how to see, even after very long periods without vision.

It seems that more destructive effects on development are involved in congenital blindness. While we do not know exactly what happens in the case of human infants, research with animals suggests that areas of the brain that are initially available and structured for vision are taken over by other functions. This has been demonstrated within the realm of vision itself. For example, the neural units in the brain that are responsible for binocular vision will become monocular units if only one eye is allowed to send visual inputs.[13] The binocular units that had accepted inputs from both eyes will be taken over completely by the eye that is sending in inputs. Similar effects have been demonstrated by biasing the input from a single eye. The projection from the eye to the brain is very orderly. If the visual input is biased, so that only one area of the eye receives any input, that part of the eye will take over areas of the brain to which it would normally not have access. These effects, whether they are measured on monkeys, cats, or frogs, occur only early in development.

There is a suggestion that similar losses can occur in the auditory system as a consequence of early undiagnosed deafness. The critical period for hearing seems to be much longer than for vision, however—perhaps as long as five years. The reason for this difference is not at present understood.

In terms of one of the major preoccupations of psychologists, the nativist-empiricist controversy, it is clear from the evidence on perceptual development that either of these extreme positions is simplistic. The perceptual system is well formed at birth, formed under genetic control. However, it develops in accordance with the information supplied to it from the environment, however biased that information may be. As we shall see in the next two chapters, this development has far-reaching effects on both motor behavior and cognitive development.

6 Motor Development

The most obvious change during the course of infancy is the baby's acquisition of new motor skills. In just a brief span of time the infant progresses from the physically helpless stage of the newborn to the point of being able to walk alone. Because these changes occur at a fairly regular rate in all infants, motor development has traditionally been attributed to maturation alone. Nonetheless, recent research has revealed that specific environmental experiences in fact play a major role in the development of motor skills. The motor development of blind babies is especially illuminating in this respect.

Motor development is the most readily observable aspect of infancy. After only a few short weeks the baby has acquired behaviors and skills that he clearly did not have at birth. These changes take place at such a regular rate that the acquisition of certain motor abilities "on schedule" is a major element in tests for normal development in infancy. The speed of development is a source of pride to some parents and a source of worry to others. A great deal of research has been invested in outlining the basis of fast or slow motor development during infancy. Motor development illustrates many of the classic problems of explaining development. We can ask meaningfully whether a particular behavior is generated by experience in the world or whether it is the result of simple maturation.

At the present I think it is safe to say that the theoretical interest in motor development is greater than its practical relevance. Accelerated motor development does not result in accelerated cognitive development. The speed with which motor skills are acquired is not predictive of the rate of acquisition of

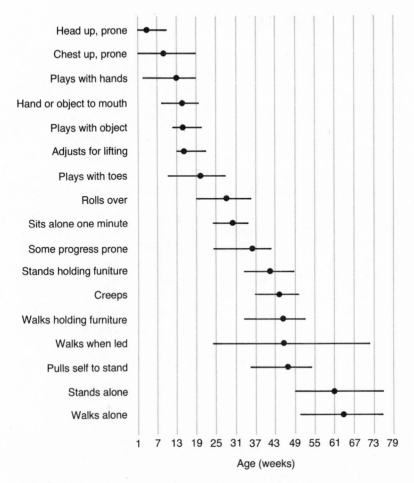

FIGURE 6.1
A schedule of motor development.

more obviously intelligent behaviors. Motor skills seem by and large to be self-contained.

Classic theories of learning have had little to say about the emergence of new motor skills and new motor capacities. They have a great deal to say about the sequence of these behaviors and the ages at which particular advances occur. The normal child, for example, will exhibit the behaviors shown in Figure 6.1 at about the ages indicated. There is little agreement, however, on the actual origins of these skills.

The Development of Walking

There are several classic studies which have led to the widespread view that motor development is maturationally determined. One is the study by Dennis of the development of walking in two groups of Hopi infants, one reared according to Hopi custom and the other not.[1] The traditionally reared Hopi baby is tied to a cradleboard and stays on the cradleboard for a fair proportion of the first nine months of life (Figure 6.2). An infant confined in this way is unable to raise his body, roll over, or move his arms. In contrast, the babies in the second group, reared in typical Western fashion, spent a large part of their time unrestricted in cribs or carriages.

This study showed that use or nonuse of the cradleboard did not affect the age at which the babies started to walk. On this basis, Dennis concluded that walking must therefore be a maturationally determined behavior, which appears by itself without the benefit of any prior behavior. However, this conclusion is not incontrovertible. Use of the cradleboard stops when babies are about nine months old, and babies do not start to walk until about the age of fifteen months. Between nine months

FIGURE 6.2
A Hopi cradleboard.

and fifteen months there are lots of opportunities for practice and function to affect the development of this motor capacity. Had the Hopi babies stayed on the cradleboard until they were fifteen months old, the maturationist case would have been stronger. As it is, all we can conclude from this study is that the restriction of movement imposed by a cradleboard does not slow development significantly, provided this restriction is limited to the first nine months of life. The effects of restriction beyond that age are completely unknown.

A conclusion of this sort is obviously far more modest than the categorical conclusion that walking is in itself maturationally determined. In fact, there is some evidence that walking is not maturationally determined, but actually does reflect the opportunities for practice and functioning that are provided. The walking behavior of newborns, described in Chapter 2, is ordinarily viewed with idle curiosity, or as an amusing party piece for the baby. In two studies this newborn capacity was systematically practiced, in one case continually and in the other case for the first two months of life.[2] In both cases the result was a tremendous acceleration of development. The infants who had been given an opportunity to practice and exercise this newborn behavior were able to walk alone and unsupported far earlier than other babies.

Newborn walking normally disappears by the eighth week. From these studies it seemed that if the behavior is used and exercised, it never truly disappears, but instead gradually turns into mature, unaided, unsupported walking. Newborn walking is genetically specified. Human newborns walk in the way they do because they are human beings. That is the way they are built. However, what happens to this behavior, how soon it turns into useful, functional, independent walking, is largely dependent upon the opportunities the environment gives the child to practice and use this built-in coordination. This would not seem to be evidence of maturational or genetic determination, but rather, evidence of maturation through environmental interaction.

Similar, but perhaps more specific, interactions of environment and gene expression occur in the development of vocalization, with the genes proposing and the environment disposing. The baby is genetically prepared to produce the sounds of any language, and young babies actually pronounce the sounds of all of them.[3] The language community in which they find themselves determines which of these sounds they will ultimately retain in their verbal repertoires. We shall examine this point further in a later chapter.

The classic studies of Arnold Gesell are also often cited as evidence that motor development is determined by maturation rather than learning. Gesell's studies involved the method of co-twin control.[4] His subjects were identical twin girls. His technique was to train only one twin in a particular motor task and then compare the performance of both babies in this task. Since the twins were genetically identical, their maturation rate, as determined by their genes, should also be identical. Thus if motor development is a matter of gene expression, then training one twin and not the other should make no difference. If, however, there is an environmental component in motor development, then the trained twin would obviously have the advantage.

What Gesell found was that his training had no effect whatsoever on the development of the various motor skills he studied. He concluded, therefore, that development of motor skills is determined primarily by maturation. This is an over-strong conclusion, given the behaviors studied. One of the learning tasks, for example, was stair climbing. One twin was trained to climb stairs, and the other was not introduced to the stairs until testing. Since the trained twin climbed no better than the untrained twin, it might seem at first glance that this ability owes nothing to practice. However, if we look at the training that was actually given, this conclusion becomes somewhat suspect. At the beginning of training, the twin was unable to climb at all. The training at that point consisted of simply lifting her passively from one tread of the stairs to the next.

Now, it seems to me that the experience of being lifted up a flight of stairs has very little to do with the ability to climb a flight of stairs actively and independently. It is far more likely that crawling on the floor, for example, was the ancestral behavior for stair climbing. That was not controlled at all. Both twins had the same opportunity to crawl about a flat surface.

The trained twin was given no more practice in plain, simple crawling than was the control twin. In other words, in this study, the special experience was not actually relevant to the criterion behavior. Under the circumstances, a conclusion that practice does not affect the performance of this behavior cannot be sustained. It is true that the particular practice that was given did not affect performance. However, in view of the nature of the practice, I don't think this was a surprising result.

The second motor task used by Gesell involved block manipulation—piling three blocks in various ways. The trained twin was given numerous chances to manipulate these blocks; the untrained twin was not. When both twins were tested, it was found that the trained twin had only a slight advantage over the untrained twin. Again, however, there was no control over manipulative experiences outside the block situation. Both twins had adequate access to other materials for manipulation. It seems quite likely that skills acquired in manipulating the materials available to both babies could very well have been transferred to the block task.

The Development of Reaching Skills

Whenever appropriate experiments have been done, it seems clear that the environment-initiated opportunities for practice in fact have a great deal to do with both the rate and direction of motor development. Consider the case of reaching and grasping, a pair of behaviors that have been the subject of a great deal of study in recent years.[5] As indicated in Chapter 2, newborns are capable of a form of reaching—not a very definitive form of reaching, but a form of reaching nonetheless. Normally this behavior disappears around the age of four weeks, and then a very similar form of behavior comes back around four months. Both these forms of reaching, which I shall call phase I reaching, are very different from a sort of reaching behavior—phase II reaching—that we typically see in six- to seven-month-old babies.

The most obvious difference between phase I and phase II reaching is in the sequencing of the components. Reaching involves the transport of the hands toward an object, or reaching proper, and closure of the hand on an object, or grasping. In phase I reaching the two components are not separated. As the young baby moves his hand toward the object, he opens it and, ideally, closes it on the object as he makes contact with it. Needless to say, there is considerable error either way, with the hand closing sometimes before it gets to the object and sometimes after it gets to the object. Nonetheless, in the average performance the hand closes just as soon as it gets to the object.

In phase II reaching, the pattern is quite different. The hand is brought to the object, that is to say, the reach proper is executed. After the hand gets to the object there is a gap of about a third of a second before closure is initiated. Reaching and grasping are thus quite widely separated. The use of the hands in phase I and phase II reaching is also quite different. Phase I reaching is typically one-handed. It is very rare to see a two-handed reach in a young baby. In phase II, two-handed reaching is very much more common.

Both these changes make the baby's reaching more functional. In the case of the one-handed reach and grasp, the hand is brought to the object, and only when the baby is sure that the hand is at the object is the grasp executed. In the case of the two-handed reach and grasp, any error made by one hand will have the effect of pushing the object toward the other hand, so that it will almost certainly be caught between the two hands. This is obviously an improvement over the one-handed phase I reach, in which any error is quite likely to knock the object completely out of range.

A second difference is that in phase I reaching the reach proper is visually initiated, but is not visually controlled, whereas in phase II reaching, it is visually initiated *and* visually controlled. What this means is that the young baby will reach out toward an object, and if his hand is launched on a miss path, so it will not contact the object, he cannot really correct his aim while the act is going on. He must withdraw his hand and start all over again. A baby capable of phase II reaching continually monitors and corrects the distance between hand and object.

In phase I reaching, grasping is visually controlled. In phase II, however, the control is tactile. For example, as noted in

Chapter 5, the young baby will reach out and close his hand on an apparently real object. The sight of the object will elicit the grasping behavior. The older babies, by contrast, do not close their hands. They stop at the object and will not grasp unless they feel some contact with it. The sight of the object is not sufficient to induce them to grasp.

What events produce all these changes in reaching behavior? It is clear that environmental factors do play a role. In one of my own experiments, babies were given daily practice in reaching for a dangling object.[6] The reason for using a dangling object was that it can be knocked away by the hand, so that an integrated reach and grasp of the phase I variety is less likely to be successful than it would be with a rigid object. What happened in this situation was that the integrated reach and grasp very soon faded away and was replaced by the separated reach-then-grasp pattern. The more mature phase II behavior appeared several weeks earlier in these babies than it did in a control group who had had no experience with dangling objects within their reach.

The experienced babies also did very much better in a situation analogous to the prism experiment described earlier. They succeeded at a younger age than the control babies in the visual monitoring of hand and object that enabled them to correct an erroneous reach. Whether this was simply because they had had much more opportunity and incentive to see their hands, and had thus habituated to their hands earlier, or whether other factors were involved is something that cannot be said at this time.

Since the shift from phase I to phase II reaching can be accelerated by a particular type of environmental intervention, can we infer that this developmental change is necessarily produced by such experiences and would not occur without them? This conclusion would seem to be too strong at the moment. In one experiment, babies were given nothing to reach for except completely rigid objects.[7] Since the rigid objects remained stationary and did not fly away when the hand got to them, there was reinforcement for the integrated reach and grasp. This arrangement did succeed in retarding the appearance of phase II reaching. However, it did not retard it permanently. The behavior emerged in any event. Whether this was due to experiences with normal objects outside the experimental situation or to processes of maturation, we simply cannot say.

In the case of reaching, all the relevant behaviors are maturationally created. The newborn is capable of grasping elicited by touch; he is capable of visually initiated reaching and grasping. But it does seem probable that environment plays a role in stitching these behaviors together into mature reaching and grasping. This is a clear case of interaction, with environmental events favoring certain built-in coordinations and discouraging others, so that a particular pattern of reaching becomes established.

The pattern that is replaced, the integrated reach and grasp, is not completely lost. In an experiment with virtual objects, it was observed that babies as old as eleven months could still produce an integrated reach and grasp. What happened was that the babies reached out to touch the image—and of course were unable to. They tried a variety of behaviors to catch the "object," and after a while, quite late in the session, some of them would let fly with an integrated reach and grasp quite like the kind of grasp babies much younger would use. Apparently the capacity, although it is not normally used at this stage, is still present and can be turned on if the situation demands it. It seems the environment selects and shapes behaviors in the short term as well as over the long term.

Motor Development in Blind Babies

The study of the motor development of the blind child is of great theoretical interest and great practical importance. There are approximately 5000 blind babies born in the United States every year. Their motor development differs from the norm for sighted babies. Perhaps because of this, their cognitive development also differs. Again, perhaps for related reasons, their personality development is different from that of sighted children. All these differences must be due to the lack of vision and to the inability of other senses to provide the information that vision normally provides. Sorting out these differences is of general importance because it allows us to define the role of vision in normal development more precisely than we can by straightforward study of the sighted. Equally important, by finding out what vision normally provides that the other senses do not, we can find some way to provide this missing information through the other senses so that they become more effective substitutes for vision.

Figure 6.3 shows the schedules of motor development for blind and sighted babies. Note that there are only two areas in which blindness seems to affect motor skills: behaviors connected with reaching and behaviors connected with independent locomotion. Blind babies are very late in reaching for noise-making objects. Some of them never attain this skill at all. Independent locomotion, walking without a human guide, is even more difficult. I have been told that as little as 10 percent of any congenitally blind population may become independently mobile. Nine out of ten blind-born babies may never walk by themselves.[8]

It is, in fact, misleading to compare schedules like those in Figure 6.3. The conditions of testing are obviously not the same, since the sighted babies can use vision and the blind babies cannot. If the sighted babies are tested in darkness, their seeming advantage disappears. Consider the development of reaching for noise-making objects in blind and sighted infants. Early in development there is no difference in many of the various hand behaviors we have described. Blind babies even indulge in hand regard, tracking their hands with their unseeing eyes.[9] Stronger evidence for the primitive, undifferentiated unity of the senses, discussed in Chapter 5, can hardly be imagined. Not surprisingly, blind babies also turn their eyes toward a sound source. Similarly, they will extend their hands to grasp the sound source. Sighted babies tested in darkness behave in exactly the same way. They look at their hands, they turn toward sound sources, and they reach out to grasp the sound source.[10] The baby's reach for a noise-making object becomes quite accurate by the age of six months. Recall, however, that this behavior then starts to decline quite sharply. Sounds became events to be listened to, rather than reached for or looked at. This is true of both the blind and the sighted baby. After this, it is a slow and

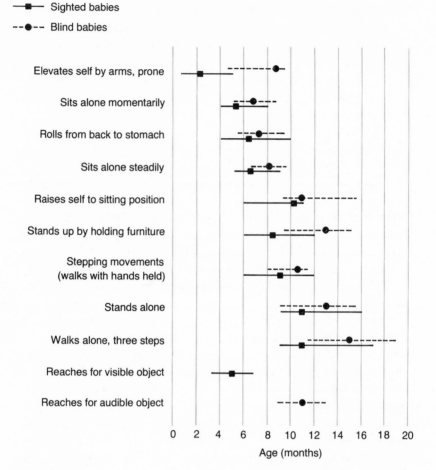

FIGURE 6.3
Comparative development of blind and sighted babies. (Data from Adelson and Fraiberg, 1974.)

painstaking process ever to reelicit reaching for unseen noise-making objects, whether in blind or sighted children.

What we have to explain, therefore, is the loss of object specification by sound that occurs at around six months. At this stage sounds no longer specify something to be looked at or touched; they have become merely events to be listened to.

There are a variety of possible explanations for this. The first, and most pessimistic, is that processes in the brain—

normal, immutable results of growth—produce the dissocia-
tion. This explanation is akin to the notion that the newborn's
capacities for walking and reaching are simply lost. Just as there
was reason to doubt the validity of the explanation there, so, I
feel, we must doubt it here, if only for its extreme pessimism. It
would imply that nothing can be done to alleviate the plight of
the blind baby.

Beside such objections on principle, there are possible
functional explanations for the decline in the use of sound to
specify object location. One of these concerns the sensory
limitations of the sounds emitted by noise-making objects. We
can discern whether a sound is coming from the right or the left
by utilizing the difference in time of arrival of the sound waves
at our ears. This is one specification that emitted sounds do
provide. However, let us look at the specifications that are not
provided by sound.

The first and least serious of these lacks is that there is no
way of immediately distinguishing between sounds coming
from directly in front of us or behind us. As Figure 6.4 shows, the
same time difference can be produced by a sound in either of
these locations. For adults this ambiguity is not serious, because
it can be resolved by a head movement. However, infants are
less able to make such head movements. Blind infants, in particular, have no way of checking visually whether they have
located the source of a sound.

The second lack in the output from sound sources is any
specification of up-down, or *azimuth*, position. There is considerable controversy over whether or not adults can pick up
azimuth position without head movements of the sort shown in
Figure 6.4. With such head movements there is no difficulty—
but again, head movements are a problem for infants.

The most serious lack in the information given by sound
sources is any information about distance. It is impossible to tell
how far away a sound source is, for anyone, adult or child.
Judgments of the distance even of familiar noise-making objects
is little better than chance in adults. With movement toward or
away from a sound source, we can pick up some information
about its distance. If a step toward a sound source doubles its
apparent loudness, we can guess its approximate distance.

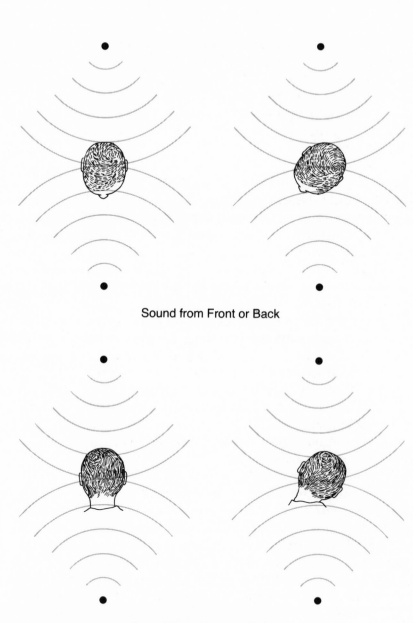

Sound from Front or Back

Sound from Above or Below

FIGURE 6.4
The only way of determining whether a sound source is in front of or behind the listener, or above or below the listener, is by moving the head to vary the time-of-arrival difference at the two ears as shown.

However, the guess is very complicated. The loudness of a sound does not change directly with distance in the way that image size does in vision. Since infants are not capable of independent locomotion anyway, the point is fairly academic.

In addition to all this missing information, there are some other problems with sound sources. First, there is nothing in a sound to specify what sort of object is emitting it. Take an obvious example, the human voice. The voice may be coming from a human face, a television set, a hi-fi speaker, or a portable radio. Only the last of these is really a graspable object for a baby; none of the others is. Second, few objects in the world actually emit sounds. The baby, blind or sighted, will continually encounter objects that do not make noises.

Let us put all this in a strictly functional context. Consider a blind baby, willing and able to reach out and grasp noise-making objects. He can tell from the sound whether the object is in his midline plane, on his right, or on his left. Suppose the noise specifies an object in the midline plane. The sound cannot specify front or back, up or down, or near or far. If it is a continuous sound, the baby has an approximate chance of figuring out the first two of these dimensions. The last is impossible. If the sound is not continuous, so that there is no opportunity to monitor it with head movements, the first two dimensions are out, perceptually, as well. Suppose the baby then reaches out. What are his chances of actually capturing the object? It must be admitted that they are very, very slight. The baby, blind or sighted, can have no inherent knowledge about precise left-right position or precise azimuth position; in particular, he can have no precise information about either the distance of the object or the length of his own arm.

The blind baby is faced with particular difficulty with respect to arm length. Space coordinates, distance, and arm length must all be precisely specified for accurate reaching. The sighted baby who reaches and misses can *see* why he has missed. He can see his hand pass above or below, before or beyond the object of interest. The sighted child thus has a means of correcting reaching errors that is not available to the blind child.

By any strictly functional account, a behavior that is reinforced as seldom as reaching for unseen noise makers must be, a behavior in which even the source of error can hardly be detected, should simply extinguish, fade out and die away—which is just what happens. Even those blind babies who do begin to reach again on sound cue do not do so in an oriented, directed way. It seems more as if the sound signals only that there is something out there somewhere. It does not signal exactly where it is. Given the limited information in emitted noises, this is not surprising.

There is another, more subtle problem raised for the blind child by presentation of noise-making objects. This is best explained by considering an experiment carried out by Held and Hein.[11] Two kittens were connected together by the apparatus shown in Figure 6.5. One kitten, the active kitten, could move voluntarily anywhere within the limits of constraint imposed by the apparatus. If it saw something interesting, it could move toward it; if it saw something aversive, it could move away from it. The kitten could use visual input to control its movements, and it could use its movements to control the visual stimuli it received. This kitten also controlled all the visual input of the other kitten. Since the passive kitten was prevented from moving independently, it received all the visual inputs provided by the movements of the active kitten. It had no control over these inputs, no way of changing them, no way of interacting with anything it saw. Its relationship to visual stimulation was completely passive, with no possibility of control through its own behavior.

When the kittens were removed from the apparatus and given a series of visual tests, the active kitten was essentially normal. The passive kitten, by contrast, simply did not react to visual stimulation at all. It could see. Its visual system was normal, but it had lost the capacity to respond to what it saw. Forced to be passive in the experimental situation, it had become passive and inactive in all situations.

Now consider the situation of the blind baby. The auditory stimulation he receives is delivered to him by others; he is a passive listener. He is, in effect, deprived of all control over the stimulation he gets. He cannot turn away from a sound that is aversive. He cannot make the sound continue if it is pleasant. In short, the blind baby is in exactly the same situation with re-

FIGURE 6.5
In this experiment the passive kitten, carried in the gondola, was exposed to essentially the same visual stimuli as the active kitten because of the unvarying pattern on the wall and the center post. The active kitten walked about more or less freely; its gross movements were transmitted to the passive kitten by the chain and bar. The only difference was in the ability of the two kittens to control the specific changes in sensory experience. Active kittens developed normal sensory-motor coordination; passive kittens failed to do so until several days after they had been freed from the apparatus. (After Held and Hein, 1963.)

spect to auditory stimulation as the passive kitten in Held's experiment was with respect to visual stimulation. Is it any wonder, then, that a blind baby becomes passive in the face of auditory stimuli that are thrust on him from the outside?

At this point, it is worth mentioning an oft-made observation about the temperament of blind babies.[12] They are very "good" babies, quiet, undemanding, even-tempered—in a word, *passive*. Is it too much to suppose that the sensory-motor passivity spreads, to become a generalized personality trait, a generalized attitude toward the world, a generalized, habitual learned helplessness?

All the above applies to one class of auditory stimuli, the sounds that come from noise-making objects. There is a whole class of auditory stimuli, however, that are not subject to any of these limitations—the stimuli that come from echoes. Suppose we make a noise with our tongue and lips. The sound waves produced by that noise radiate out from our mouth, and bounce back from any object in their path. The echoes produced in this way contain a great deal of information that sounds emitted by objects do not. Let us see just what this information is.

The first and most important dimension provided by echoes is distance. Since sound travels at a constant speed, the farther away an object is, the longer will its echo take to reach the ear (Figure 6.6). The relationship is perfectly predictable. It is a better indicator of distance than any visual stimulus, treated purely as a stimulus. Second, echoes specify the radial direction of objects. The echo from an object on the right reaches the right ear before the left ear, and vice-versa, just the same as sound waves emitted from an object. An echo does not specify azimuth position. However, if one is *producing* the sounds that make the echoes, and can do so in coordination with head movements, then it is possible to discover the azimuth position of an object without difficulty.

An echo can also specify the size of an object. The larger the object, the more of the sound wave it will reflect back. This variable, in conjunction with distance specification, permits accurate determination of size at any distance. Echoes can even specify, to some extent, the shape of an object, although the specification is far from precise.

What is the relevance of echoes to blind babies? Well, it has been known for some years that those blind adults who are mobile use echoes to obtain the information they use to navigate.[13] They use echoes from their footsteps, echoes from a tapping cane, echoes made by snapping their fingers, and so on. Echoes of this sort may not always be available. However, if a blind person is provided with an automatic clicker that pro-

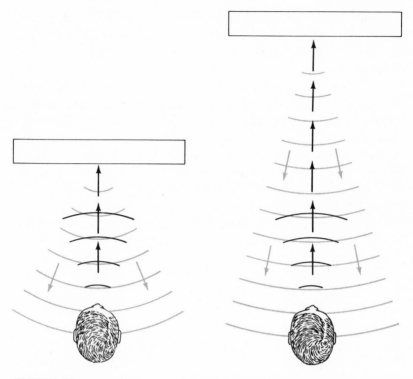

FIGURE 6.6
An echo specifies the distance of an object by the time interval between the output of a sound and the return of this sound as an echo.

duces more precise echoes than the natural devices above, his ability to orient himself in his surroundings becomes more precise. In recent years further research has been done on even more precise echo-location devices.

Suppose a blind baby were capable of utilizing echoes. What opportunity would he have to do so? In the usual home environment, unfortunately, he would have precious little. The baby cannot produce echoes by tapping his heel or snapping his fingers. The only source spontaneously available to him is his voice. However, his environment will not usually be quiet enough or have the sort of furnishings that allow registration of these echoes. In a home furnished with radio, television, and the customary electrical appliances, and with carpets and drapes designed specifically to absorb sound, there is not much opportunity to use the kinds of echoes a baby can produce. The subtle information in the echoes will be swamped by the overall ambient noise.

Does this matter? Is there any evidence that babies, blind or sighted, can use echoes? In the case of one blind baby there is some evidence.[14] I was fortunate enough to be allowed to test this infant when his age was effectively six weeks.* At that time his behavioral repertoire was quite large. His vocalizations were strange, too, in that he produced an inordinate number of sharp, clicking noises with his lips and tongue. I had never heard a sighted baby make such noises. I made the guess that these noises were intended to produce echoes. To test this, I dangled a large ball in front of the baby, completely silently. The baby turned to "look" at it. I moved the ball, again silently. After a vocalization interval of clicks, he turned to follow it.

This performance was repeated seven times. All the movements of the ball were completely silent. The performance was spectacular enough to move one member of the audience to doubt the diagnosis of blindness. Another spontaneously produced the echo-location explanation. It seemed clear that this baby could use the echoes he produced to locate objects.

The echo-location idea was explained to the baby's parents, and they were asked to make sure he had an opportunity to continue to make use of this ability. They did so by arranging toys over his crib. The position of the toys was changed every time the baby was put in. All the toys were noise makers of some sort and would make a noise when struck or pulled. The baby learned quite quickly that when he was put in his crib there would be a toy somewhere for him to play with. However, the only way he could find it would be to use echoes. He succeeded in doing this. By the (corrected) age of sixteen weeks, he could reliably find any fairly large object dangled over his crib. He was able to generalize this ability to other situations to some extent.

---

*The baby's chronological age was sixteen weeks. However, he was ten weeks premature, so that his conceptual age, or age from conception, was forty-six weeks, making him equivalent to a normal six-week-old.

At this age the baby was equipped with a very sophisticated echo-location device that could produce echoes from objects as small as a knitting needle. It also operated continuously, without requiring activity by the baby, so that he was free to use his vocalizations for other purposes. When the baby was first fitted with this device, he did not make anything of it. However, within a few minutes the following observations were made. When an object was moved to and from the baby's face, convergent and divergent eye movements were observed, something the baby had never done before. Side-to-side movement elicited quite accurate swiping movements of the hands at the object.

At the time of writing this baby is six months old. He can reach accurately, using two hands, to capture silent objects. He can recognize and distinguish two silent objects from any others. One is his bottle, to which he responds by opening his mouth before the bottle gets there. The other is a favorite toy. In this case the recognition is shown by his continual willingness to reach out and take that toy, while refusing to take others. This behavior is also integrated smoothly and efficiently with the game he plays with this toy: he puts its textured side against his cheek and presses it to make it squeak. When the favorite toy is presented, the sequence of two-handed reach and grasp, followed by transfer to one hand, and then retraction of the hand to insert the texture against his cheek, goes off very smoothly, as one integrated act. This would not be possible without prior recognition of the toy.

It is, of course, far too early to say whether or not this skill will persist. Nonetheless, these first results are highly encouraging. This baby can do things with the aid of the echo-sounding device that are more typical of a sighted than a blind baby. At this point, too, it can fairly be said that the baby is not at all passive in his interactions with the world.

There seems to be a dependence between reaching and locomotion in the blind. Without some channel of information to tell him that there is a solid surface out there that will support him, the blind child is stepping into a complete void. All that was said above about the specification of objects to reach for applies with greater force to the specification of surfaces to stand on. The basic problem is one of sensory supplementation.

Motor Development
in Down's Syndrome

Retarded motor development is characteristic of other handicapping developmental conditions. One such case is *Down's syndrome,* a genetic defect caused by the presence of an extra chromosome. The Down's baby typically takes twice as long to develop any motor skills as a normal child does. Because this condition is the result of an extra chromosome, it has long been assumed that the retardation was inevitable and irreversible. This does not seem to be so.

There have been two studies to this end. In one massive study, Down's babies at the age of two were given intensive practice on a number of sensory-motor tasks.[15] At two, these babies were like normal one-year-olds. By the age of three-and-a-half, after eighteen months of practice, they had the motor and manipulation skills of normal three-and-a-half-year-olds. It is not known whether this boost in manipulative intelligence will transfer to other domains of cognitive ability. The second study focused on only one baby.[16] The baby was given operant control over an object in his environment. This raised his activity level, accelerated his smiling, and accelerated his reaching skill to a level that was precocious even for normal babies.

What these studies show, I think, is that even when there is a genetic abnormality, suitable environmental manipulations can boost development to a normal level, in some respects at least. The limitations of these boosts are currently unknown. However, the reversals that have been demonstrated are spectacular enough that it would seem well worthwhile to pursue this line of research. Where development is handicapped either by an environmental loss, as in the case of blindness, or by a genetic abnormality, as in the case of Down's syndrome, suitable modifications of the environment can, apparently, ease the burden of the handicap to a considerable extent. This surely argues for the importance of the environment in all of motor development.

7 Cognitive Development

Some of the most surprising findings about babies concern the cognitive development that takes place during infancy. Although such concepts as number and conservation are usually thought to develop around the age of three or four, long after the child has learned to speak, infants demonstrate these concepts at a functional level by the time they are a year old. By this time they have also acquired such basic concepts as an understanding of objects, spatial relationships, weight, and causality. The age at which these concepts appear is somewhat plastic, and each cognitive advance seems to depend on a conflict between two or more previously developed responses which must be resolved in a problem-solving situation.

Cognitive development is perhaps the busiest and most important area of development in the human infant. We somehow do not think of young babies as intellectual. As a result, the idea that infants derive intellectual pleasure from solving problems may seem a startling notion. Nonetheless, as we saw in Chapter 3, babies smile vigorously when they discover the solution to a new problem. There is additional evidence that they do indeed learn for the pleasure of learning.

The Pleasures of Learning

The fact that babies are fascinated by problems is, I think, demonstrated quite clearly by experiments such as the following. Papousek showed babies a tiny light display which they could switch on by making the correct head turn.[1] He found that the babies would engage in a fair amount of movement until they had figured out how to turn on the light; then the frequency of the head movements would drop. When the contingency was changed, so that a different head movement was needed to switch on the light, the babies would sooner or later notice that things had been changed, and then there would be a big burst of activity accompanied by intense smiling when the baby found out the correct coordination—and then a drop in activity. If the contingency was again changed, the behavior would again pick up until the baby had solved the problem.

The babies, as Papousek described them, were intensely interested, fascinated by this game, and derived a good deal of pleasure from it. The pleasure was not in the light; the babies scarcely looked at the light. They only glanced at it to see if they had figured things out or not. It was the solving of the problem that motivated them. As long as there was a problem to be solved, they would perform in this situation. Once they had solved the problem, so that all that was left was to switch on the boring light, they simply did not bother to try to do so.

It is extremely interesting and quite important that problem solving is, in itself, motivating for babies, that they will act to solve problems. In a sense, this means that we don't have to search for ways to make babies learn or acquire knowledge. They want to do so for the pleasure that it gives them.

There have been many attempts to describe the changes in cognitive functioning that take place during infancy. The learning process itself undergoes considerable change. Monnier conducted an experiment similar to Papousek's, in which babies could control a mobile by moving their arms or legs.[2] Each arm and each leg was connected to the apparatus, and the baby's problem was to find out which leg or arm would actually operate the mobile. Younger babies, at about four months, found the solution simply by engaging in a great deal of activity. The successful arm or leg was discovered, it seemed, more or less by chance. Older babies, however, approached the problem quite systematically, trying first one arm, then the other arm, then one leg, and then the other leg. If the contingency was changed, so that the previously successful arm or leg was no longer successful, they would repeat this performance, until they found out which member was responsible.

In another phase of the experiment, the task could be made more difficult by requiring combinations of movement. The babies in this experiment, who were about nine months or more, were apparently able to cope with such a problem. They would systematically move both arms, both legs, one arm and one leg, the other arm and the other leg, the other arm and one leg, the one arm and the other leg. They were able to dissect their own movements and combine them in various permutations to find out which one was actually operative in this situation.

While these changes in problem-solving capacity are extremely fascinating and potentially very important, they have only recently been described, and we do not yet have any real idea of their basis. Whether changes in learning ability are determined by environmental experiences, by maturation alone, or by a combination of the two is something we do not know, for the requisite studies have not been done.

The Development
of the Object Concept

One area which has been intensively studied is the development of the object concept, a segment of development which takes up a large part of the baby's life. It is very clear that young babies do not think of objects in the same way we do. Rather, they appear to identify an object in terms of either its location or its motion.[3] A baby seems unable to understand that the same object can appear in different places, or that different objects can appear in the same place. He also does not seem to understand that an object must move in order to get from one place to another.

For example, suppose a baby is presented with some object—say, a toy train—that moves from the center of the track to the right, stops for a moment, then moves back to the center, and after a stop at the center, moves back to the right, and so on. The whole event is completely visible. Within a few trials, babies of twelve weeks can track the object from the center to the right and back again perfectly accurately. They seem to understand very well what is going on.

But look what happens when the object is moved to a new place; after a stop at the center, instead of going right, the object goes to the left. What the babies do is turn and look back to the right, where they had previously seen the object. They seem very surprised indeed to see nothing there, even though the object is in plain sight on the left. As far as these babies are concerned, there are two stationary objects, one in front of them and one on the right. They do not associate the object in the center with the one on the right, or with the movement from one place to the other. When the object in the center disappeared—or rather moved off to the left—they turned to inspect the stationary object on the right, apparently not realizing that there would be nothing there.

The same lack of conceptual knowledge can be observed when babies are shown a moving object that has stopped. When this happens, the babies will stop, too, and look at the stationary object. But, perhaps because they find the moving object more interesting, they will then search for the moving object along the path on which it was moving, even though the stationary object is right there in front of them. They do not seem to understand the transition from moving to stopped—that only one object is involved. They do not comprehend that it means there is no more moving object.

Even more bizarre are the things that are totally unsurprising to a young baby. For example, if young babies are shown a moving object that simply disappears in the middle of its trajectory, they are quite unconcerned. An invisible movement does not bother them at all.[4] Similarly, if they are shown a stationary object that is tranformed to one that looks completely different (Figure 7.1), they do not seem to be particularly surprised; they certainly do not look around for the original object. Indeed, this latter behavior often doesn't appear until well into the second half of the first year of life. Somewhere between four and five months, babies begin to amalgamate their ideas about objects and realize that an object is a single entity that can move from place to place.

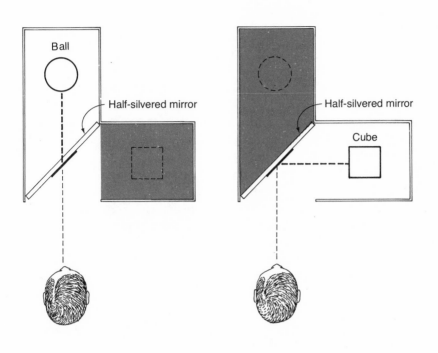

Ball

Half-silvered mirror

Half-silvered mirror

Cube

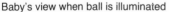

Baby's view when ball is illuminated   Baby's view when cube is illuminated

FIGURE 7.1
When the tunnel containing the ball is illuminated and the tunnel on the right is dark, the baby sees the ball through the half-silvered mirror. If this light is put out at exactly the same moment the tunnel containing the cube is illuminated, the baby sees the ball mysteriously transformed into a cube.

One quite dramatic experiment which shows this advancing knowledge was carried out by Mundy-Castle and Anglin.[5] Babies were shown an object moving up in one window and then, after a fixed interval, moving down in an adjacent window, then up again in the first window, and so on (Figure 7.2). Young babies simply transfer their gaze from window to window, or else tracked the object to the ceiling or the floor, continuing the path of movement.

However, somewhere between the age of four and five months there is a new development. The babies start to interpolate a trajectory between the disappearance of the object at the top of one window and its reappearance at the top of the other,

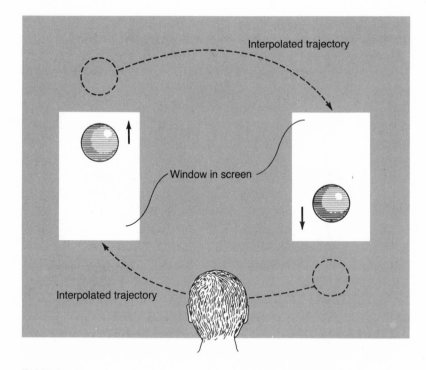

FIGURE 7.2
When babies are shown an object moving upward in one window and then descending in the other window, they will track the object on its path of movement and then interpolate the trajectory it is most likely to be following during the time it is hidden from view. (After Mundy-Castle and Anglin, 1969.)

and between its disappearance at the bottom of that window and its reappearance at the bottom of the other. These trajectories were quite precise. They were determined by the speed of movement of the object and the length of time the object was out of sight. The babies seemed to know that for the object to get from one place to another it must pass along a certain trajectory, and they would look along that trajectory to see if the object was perhaps visible at any point on this path.

A second demonstration of this change in knowledge is the baby's response to the appearance of multiple mothers (Figure 7.3). If we are right in thinking that young babies do not realize that a single object can appear in many places, it follows that the baby must think he has multiple mothers, one for each place in which he commonly sees his mother. So, what happens then if we show him three mothers all at once? A baby of less than five months is not at all surprised. In fact, he seems quite delighted and will interact with all three mothers in turn.

This happy state does not last. The situation for a baby over five months is quite different. When he sees three simultaneously visible mothers, he is quite shocked and will protest. Having worked out that he has only one mother, and that it is the same mother that he sees everywhere he goes, it must be rather disconcerting to see three of them all together in a room, all looking at him.

A baby's discovery that he has only one mother also seems to affect his relationship with her. It is only after he has come to the realization that he has one and only one mother that the baby will protest vigorously at his mother's disappearance. Prior to that point, babies seem to think that if one mother goes, another one will pop up somewhere.

Development of the perceptual system may be important in determining this aspect of cognitive development. When the baby's perceptual system is sufficiently matured and sufficiently experienced that he can recognize the identity of an object seen in different places, it becomes more economical for him to identify things by their features, rather than their locations. Once a baby notices that an object in place B is the same as or identical with an object that was in place A, he has to work out how it got from place A to place B. This must facilitate the

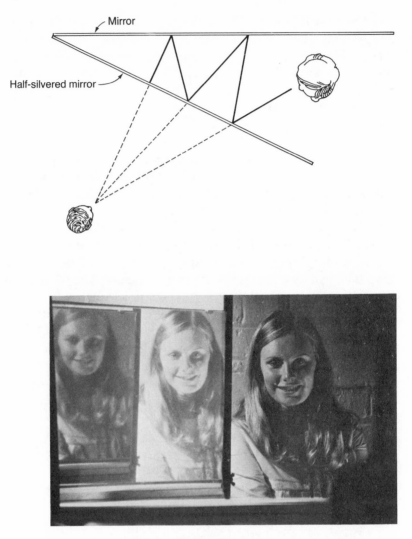

Baby's view of multiple mothers

FIGURE 7.3

A young baby does not find the appearance of multiple mothers in the least disturbing and will interact with each one in turn. With increasing understanding of object identity, the simultaneous appearance of three mothers is most disconcerting. This change occurs at around the age of five months. (After Bower, 1974; photo by Jane Dunkeld.)

coordination of place and movement, a development that obviously makes the baby's life much simpler. He has far fewer objects to deal with once he recognizes that many of the objects he sees are actually the same object seen in different places.

The Concept of Spatial Relationships

Given that a five-month-old has stuck place and movement together, and knows that objects can get from place to place along a trajectory, and can, indeed, work out what this trajectory might be, what does he still not comprehend? The baby still has no grasp of the spatial relationships between one object and another. Suppose a baby is shown an attractive toy and this toy is then placed on top of a platform. The baby could be in mid-reach for the toy. When it is placed on top of the platform, he will pull back his hand and look at the toy in bewilderment (Figure 7.4). He may grasp the platform and accidentally knock

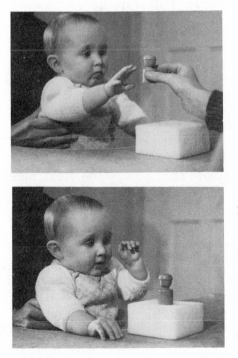

FIGURE 7.4
This baby is obviously puzzled by the relationship *on*. The difficulty of this concept depends on how much common boundary the two objects have. A ball, for example, would be easier for the baby to see as a separate object than this toy with a flat bottom. (Photos by Jennifer G. Wishart.)

the toy off; but he doesn't seem to realize that the toy could be removed from the platform all by itself. He doesn't seem to realize that one object can be on top of another.

This confusion is more clearly demonstrated if we use two platforms. If we place an object on the first platform, the baby might shake the object off and thereby succeed in retrieving it. If we place it back on the same platform, he will shake it off again and retrieve it. Suppose on the third trial we put the toy on the other platform. What does the baby do? What he does is shake the first platform. He repeats the particular response which brought him the toy before, not actually realizing at all the connection between the spatial relationships of the objects and their accessibility.[6]

The baby has exactly the same problem with the spatial relation *in*. If we show a baby an attractive toy and then place it inside a covered cup or other container, the baby will act completely amazed. He may eventually remove the cover and retrieve the toy, but it is most obvious that he doesn't comprehend the spatial relations involved at all. This is apparent if we use a variant of the test above, with two cups. If the toy is placed in one cup, the baby may successfully retrieve it; when it is again placed in the same cup, he will retrieve it in the same way. However, on the third trial, if the toy is now placed in the other cup, the baby still goes to the cup in which he had previously found the toy. He does this even if the cups used are transparent. With a transparent cup, just as with a platform, the toy is truly in view. A clearer demonstration of the magical way the child thinks about the world can hardly be given.

It is clear then that the child of five, six, seven, eight, nine months doesn't understand the spatial relationships *on* and *in*. How about the relationships *in front of* and *behind*? These have been studied as well. If a baby is shown an object in front of another, larger object, he has no difficulty in reaching out and taking the smaller object in front of the larger one. If, however, the distance between the desirable toy and the larger object is steadily decreased until there is no perceptible separation, he has just as much difficulty as with an object he sees on top of or inside another object.

FIGURE 7.5
Under the condition shown here, the relationship *behind* is no problem for the baby. (Photo by Jennifer G. Wishart.)

The same thing happens with the concept *behind*. If one object is well behind another object, a baby of five months or so has no difficulty in going around the occluding object to take the desired object (Figure 7.5). In some cases he will pick up the occluding object and throw it away. However, if the distance between the two objects is short, so that there is again no perceptible separation, he is just as helpless as in the preceding situations. It seems that what the baby doesn't understand is that two objects can be in spatial relationship to one another, so that they share a common boundary. Evidently it is the common boundary that is critical. Babies have much less difficulty with an object such as a ball, which really can have no common boundary with another object. At any age when spatial relationships are a problem, they are far more likely to succeed with a ball than with a cube, or a half-ball, for example.

This inability to comprehend spatial relationships shows up in another task as well. Suppose we present the baby with a desirable toy that is out of reach, but is on top of some other object, such as a cloth, which is within his reach. He will try to get the toy by pulling on the cloth. By the age of six months babies will make use of these intermediaries as tools. If, however, the desirable toy is not actually on the cloth, but is merely beside it, he will still pull on the object that is within reach and will be disappointed that he has not succeeded in gaining the toy (Figure 7.6). Again, this is simply lack of comprehension of spatial relations and their consequences ftr objects. A baby will ordinarily be ten months old before he can pass this particular test.[7]

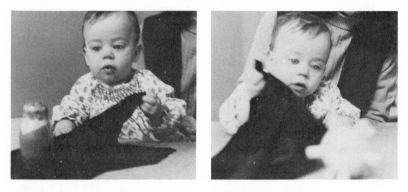

FIGURE 7.6
If an object is placed on a cloth such that the object is out of reach, the baby will pull the cloth in to obtain the object. If, however, an object is placed out of reach but to the side of the cloth, the baby still pulls in the cloth, fully expecting to be successful again. The use of a cloth to get an object that is out of reach is still "magic" at this age; the baby does not understand the spatial relations necessary between cloth and object for this strategy to work. (Photos by Jennifer G. Wishart.)

Even at this point, the comprehension of spatial relations is incomplete, and in a sense still magical. Suppose we show a ten- or eleven-month-old baby a toy, place the toy in one of the two cups, and then transpose the cups. If the toy has been hidden in the cup on the right, and the baby has seen this cup transposed to the left, he will nevertheless look in the cup that is now on the right. He will look in the place he had seen the toy placed, ignoring the transposition of the cups. He doesn't seem to realize that the toy in the cup shares in all the movements of that cup; it stands in a container-contained relationship. There are similar difficulties with the other concepts in this category.

Eventually the baby will solve even this task, but his comprehension of spatial relationships is still not complete. Consider the problem shown in Figure 7.7. The baby sees a toy hidden in the center cup. However, instead of moving the cup, suppose we now move the baby, so that the cup that was previously in the center is now on the baby's right. What does the baby do? He chooses the center cup. He doesn't seem to realize that his own change of position has changed the spatial relations of the objects in front of him.

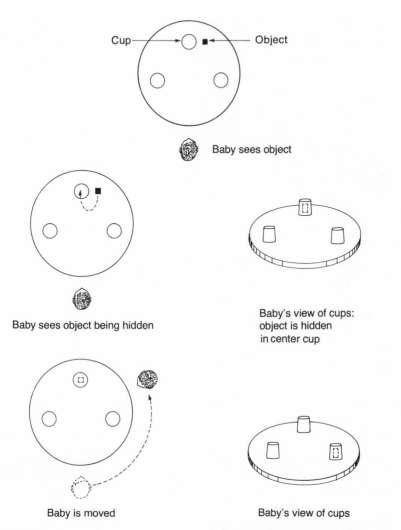

Cup ——— ○ ■ ——— Object

Baby sees object

Baby sees object being hidden

Baby's view of cups:
object is hidden
in center cup

Baby is moved

Baby's view of cups

FIGURE 7.7
Problems of this kind are very difficult for babies. The baby saw the object being hidden under the center cup, but after he had been moved around the table, it was then in the cup on his right. He makes no allowance for his change in position, however, and searches for the object in the cup which is now in the center.

This kind of behavior is commonly described as egocentric. Others prefer to say that the child has a set of absolute descriptions of objects and doesn't realize that in some cases absolute descriptions are inappropriate. An object that is on his right may no longer be on his right when he moves. With a change in his own position, what was on his right may be on his left, in the middle, or elsewhere. The baby doesn't seem to appreciate the relativism of spatial relations until he is about eighteen months old.

The Concepts and the Cup

This absolutism and unawareness of relativity, while it is most obvious in these object-concept problems, seems to plague the baby in a number of other contexts. Consider the ordinary task of drinking out of a cup. Bruner has beautifully described the dreadful problem that cups present for young babies.[8] At first the baby doesn't really comprehend the relationship between the angle of the cup and behavior of the liquid it contains. He seems to imagine that liquid will come out of the cup more or less as a solid gout and simply turns the cup up when he gets it to his face. The inevitable result (Figure 7.8) may be amusing enough for the baby, but is not very effective from the standpoint of drinking.

Before the age of one year, the baby has worked out the complex relationship between liquid level, gravity, and the edge of a cup. Babies of this age can drink smoothly and efficiently. They simply pick up the cup and tip it to the required angle. However, their absolutism shows in another situation. Suppose we show a year-old baby some milk in a transparent container, pour the milk into a narrower, opaque container, and allow the

FIGURE 7.8
The ten-month-old baby is likely to misjudge the angle necessary for drinking, which requires a grasp of the complex relationships between the behavior of liquids, gravity, and the edge of the cup. (Photo by Jennifer G. Wishart.)

baby to drink from that. Evidently babies think the milk will be at the same height in the narrower container, and so they tip it accordingly, again with the inevitable result. Similarly, if the liquid is transferred to a wider opaque container, so that the level is lower, they are disappointed, because when they tip the glass, nothing comes into their mouth. They seem to imagine that liquid levels stay constant and are independent of the shape of the container the liquid is in.

Once again, this should remind us of the baby's inability to appreciate relationships between the container and the contained. Babies get over this problem around the age of fifteen months, and can cope when their milk or juice is transposed from a glass of one shape to another. There is an intermediate stage in which the baby must look at the liquid level to know where it is. By the age of fifteen months they don't need to look at it. If they are prevented from doing so, by a lid on the cup, they can still drink smoothly and efficiently without any difficulty at all.[9]

The Concepts of Conservation and Number

The same absolutism shows in the kind of problem illustrated in Figure 7.9. When babies are shown a set of cups piled in a tier on the floor, they have great difficulty in reproducing

FIGURE 7.9
At less than three weeks infants are beginning to adjust their grasp to the size of a single object, and by six months they are very good at it. However, one-year-olds and even some two-year-olds cannot arrange this series of cups according to size.

this arrangement. Typically, what they do is take a big cup and a small cup and pair them. They seem to classify the objects only as big or small, an absolutist judgment. Big, bigger, biggest or small, smaller, smallest, which are relativistic judgments, are exceedingly difficult for babies, although they do master them during the period of infancy.[10]

Another example of absolutism is the baby's judgment of weight. The very young baby expects all objects to weigh the same. He goes from this to a predictive relativism, assuming that the longer an object is, the heavier it will be. Here, again, he does not take account of the relationship of width and length to weight, which leads to strange errors. If he is handed a long, thin object, he is likely to expect it to weigh much more than it does and will tense his muscles accordingly. If he is handed a very short, wide object, he will anticipate its weight on the basis of length alone, and his arm may sag under a weight he didn't expect.

However, by the time a baby is eighteen months old, he does take account of both dimensions. He also knows that the weight of an object is independent of changes in its shape. A ball of plasticine can turn into a sausage which weighs the same. What this means is that the baby has attained the concept of conservation of weight. The realization that weight is invariant under shape change is a very late attainment if we measure it verbally; the baby, however, attains this concept nonverbally, as expressed in his behavior, by the age of eighteen months.[11]

By this age babies have acquired other complex concepts that are unexpected, such as the concept of number. If we present babies with choice tasks like those shown in Figure 7.10, the young baby will have no consistent success in actually selecting the larger number of candies. Sometimes he goes by the density of the arrangement, at other times he seems to go by its length. However, by the age of eighteen months he is quite capable of going through all the tasks shown and consistently picking the larger number. The only way this is possible—and the way the baby seems to do it—is by actually making one-to-one correspondences between the two arrays and picking the one that has the greater number, regardless of density, length, or spac-

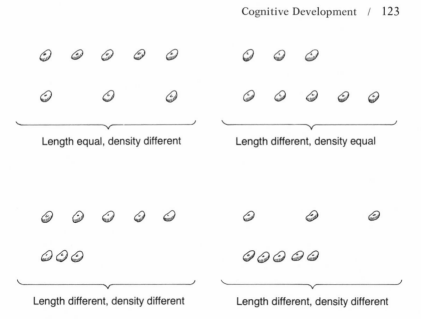

FIGURE 7.10
By the age of eighteen months babies are able to solve these choice problems by making a one-to-one correspondence between the objects in each group. In other words, these babies are actually "counting," even though the "numbers" as yet have no names.

ing.[12] This, again, is a very high level attainment for a baby, because verbally at least, a child will probably be five or six before he can solve these tasks with equal fluency.

Mechanisms of Cognitive Development

What is it that impels the baby through this sequence of development? How is it that a baby starts with no comprehension even that an object can move from place to place, and yet develops during infancy to the point of being able to count, estimate weight, even know that weight is invariant under transformation, and understand fairly well all the possible spatial relationships between objects? What are the forces that produce these changes?

The greatest amount of work that has been done on the factors producing development has been in connection with the object concept, so let us return to this topic. A first answer would be that the baby simply becomes mechanically more skillful as he gets older. Certainly the role of motor skill in all these tasks should not be underestimated. However, motor development has its limits; there is a point beyond which we are not talking about motor development, but about the control of established motor behavior. It seems that in most of the cognitive areas we have considered in this chapter, the requisite motor skill has appeared before the concept is attained. The control or use of the motor skill still has to be developed. This is what we call cognitive development.

There is another argument against the role of motor development in concept formation. Babies who have insurmountable motor handicaps still go through the same sequence of cognitive development, at about the same rate. The most striking instances of this are thalidomide babies who have, for example, no arms. When these babies are tested in object-concept tasks like those described above, they get the objects with their teeth.[13] They move the cups with their teeth, pull strings with their teeth. These babies obviously cannot have had the experiences, and motor experiences in particular, that normal babies have. Nonetheless, they develop what seems to be a normal object concept. It seems that there are very many different routes to the same developmental end.

A further point which must be noted is that, while development of the object concept normally takes about eighteen months, the process can be considerably accelerated, and bits of the process can be omitted, without affecting the breadth and level of development. Since babies are intelligent and enjoy problem-solving situations, one might think that the best way to accelerate or promote this learning process is simply to present the babies with the requisite problems and allow them to get on and solve them. The possibility of acceleration by this means has limits which are quite difficult to define. In one sense it seems that we can expect a baby to solve a problem and to produce a developmental advance only if he has already acquired the elements of the solution, and has simply not yet put them together.

Consider one of the various bits of the object concept, learning that a single object can move from place to place along a trajectory. It is possible to accelerate this discovery by giving the baby intensive practice in tracking objects. If we show a baby an object that moves and stops, stops and moves, and so on, sooner or later he will work out that there is really only one object involved, and that it is moving from place to place. He will learn to track it appropriately, without the error either of continuing to look for the moving object or of looking in the familiar place for the stationary object.

However, we can actually delay development if we introduce the baby to this problem too early. The young baby is described as making two "errors," but in fact, these are strategies of finding things to look at in the world. The two errors, or two strategies, as I prefer to call them, develop at different times. Looking for things in familiar places typically emerges first. The ability to follow along a path of movement emerges later, possibly because the baby's perceptual system doesn't register motion too efficiently in the early weeks, and possibly because the baby doesn't have the motor control to make these smooth movements. As a result, the small baby typically does not track an object smoothly when it is moving. When the object moves, he will turn to a place where he might expect to see it, but will make very little attempt to follow the movement itself.

By the age of twelve weeks the ability to follow moving objects and the readiness to continue to follow them after they have stopped is well established. Only at this point is it profitable to introduce practice. If it is introduced before this point, development will be retarded. The babies will find the problem too much for them. They will not have the two possible responses in their repertoire—place-to-place following and movement following—and so will be unable to combine them to come to an accurate solution.

All we do by giving babies a problem before they are ready for it is to make the whole situation a vexation for them. As a result, they will tend to avoid the entire problem context and will fuss and try to look away when presented, for example, with any tracking task.

It seems that what we must have for a correct solution is a *conflict* between two possible ways of responding to a situation. In a tracking situation the baby is in a conflict between his moving-object strategy and his stationary-object strategy. At any time in tracking an object that moves and stops, the baby has a choice of either his place-to-place strategy or his movement strategy. With each of them he will be wrong some of the time. But if he is using both together, they are inevitably in conflict. Whenever an object that has been moving stops or a stationary object begins to move, the baby is in conflict. It is this conflict more than anything else that seems to be required for acceleration to occur. The baby's resolution of such conflicts goes through several stages. The particular stage of resolution determines whether he will transfer the appropriate information from one problem situation to another.

Both these points are clear from the following experiment.[14] The objective was to accelerate the development of trajectory interpolation in the situation illustrated in Figure 7.2. The babies were presented with two tracking problems, shown in Figure 7.11. In the first situation an object simply moved and stopped at various points on a horizontal track in front of the baby. In the other situation the object did not stop but moved continuously on a circular path that passed behind a screen.

It is clear that the first arrangement is a conflict situation for the twelve-week-old baby. When the stationary object moves and then stops, the baby is in a conflict between using his place-to-place tracking behavior and his movement tracking behavior. This conflict leads, initially, at least, to acceleration of learning. The baby seems to decide that what is happening here is that an object is moving from place to place along a trajectory. When these babies were presented with the Mundy-Castle situation in Figure 7.2, they interpolated trajectories between the two places where the object appeared. They saw this as an instance of an object moving from place to place, and they searched for the object along its trajectory.

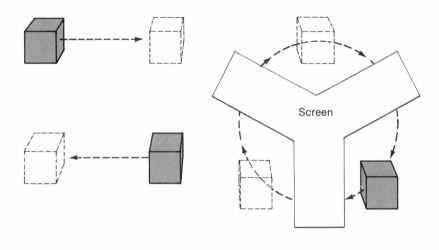

Side-to-Side Tracking   Continuous Tracking on Trajectory

FIGURE 7.11
Side-to-side tracking presents a conflict situation, since the baby sees the object both moving on a trajectory and stopped for a moment in each place. In the other training situation, the object moves continuously on a circular trajectory, passing behind the Y-shaped screen. Since the object is never seen as stationary, the only possible response is tracking it along its trajectory. (Data from Bower, 1976.)

The second situation is not a conflict situation, because the object is never stationary. It simply continues on its trajectory behind the screen. What we would expect, therefore, is reinforcement of the tendency to search for objects along the path of motion on which they had been seen. And so we would expect what actually happened. When these babies were presented with the Mundy-Castle situation, they followed the object up, up, up, beyond the window, until their gaze was virtually at the ceiling. When they caught sight of the descending object, they tracked the descent all the way down to the floor. There was no interpolation of a trajectory between the two appearances of the object. The babies simply transferred from one situation to the other the strategy that had been reinforced, the strategy of searching for a moving object along its trajectory.

However, with greater exposure to the two tracking situations in Figure 7.11, the pattern reversed somewhat. After being shown the side-to-side tracking for long enough, the babies in this group seemed to change their rule to something of the following sort: "to keep in contact with an object that is moving, simply track from side-to-side in a horizontal plane." And this is what they did in the Mundy-Castle situation, using very square-looking eye movements, which were actually quite efficient, but which did not show the conceptual knowledge required for trajectory interpolation. By contrast, after lengthy exposure to the circular tracking, the babies in this group began to respond essentially like naïve infants, no longer making the vast up-and-down excursions. Presumably this was because they had specialized the solution to the circular-tracking task and recognized that the Mundy-Castle task was completely different and so, perhaps, required a different kind of response. The important point, however, is that the conflict situation of side-to-side tracking, given in the right dose, did produce accelerated development.

What of the later stages of the object concept? Here again babies seem to be able to pick up the requisite information from situations other than the given test situation. It has been found that suitable tracking experiences will teach a baby that an object can be put on top of another object, or inside another object, and still be an available object (Figure 7.12).[15] In this case, too, there seems to be a necessary conflict involved. The baby is shown what to him is a mysterious event, such as an object going inside a tunnel and then coming out. He can accept this as an incomprehensible event, but it becomes a conflict for him when he reaches the stage of development at which he begins to identify objects in terms of their features.

This requires certain perceptual advances, as discussed above, but once the baby gets to this point, so that he can identify objects in terms of the way they look rather than where they are, then the object that goes into a tunnel can be seen as identical to the object that comes out of a tunnel. Does the baby then decide he is dealing with two objects which just happen to be identical, or does he take the enormous simplifying step of realizing that he is dealing with a single object which must therefore still exist inside the tunnel? It seems clear from many experiments that what the baby does is decide that there is only one object involved.

Visual Tracking
of Object

Reaching Tasks

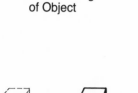

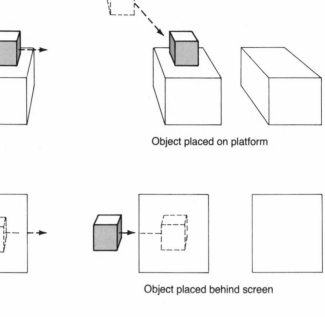

Object placed on platform

Object placed behind screen

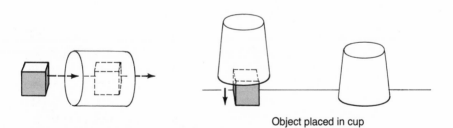

Object placed in cup

FIGURE 7.12
Practice in the tracking tasks on the left accelerated performance in the reaching tasks on the right. (Data from Wishart and Bower, 1976*b*).

The best evidence of this is that babies given some experience with the tracking tasks shown in Figure 7.12 were able to transfer their learning perfectly to the situation of an object and two platforms or two cups, described earlier. However, it is again important to note that the transfer task had to be presented quite early if it was to be successful. If babies were given too long a period of tracking experience, then they did not transfer the concept to a new test situation. It seems that the babies could develop a very specific strategy for coping with the tracking situation—a strategy that was highly efficient in that situation but became too specialized for transfer to a new one. Only while solutions to the tracking tasks were somewhat abstract, and not specific in terms of stimulus and response, was there any real possibility of transfer, or so the results would indicate.

In these various experiments the important element seems to be conflict between two responses that the baby has acquired independently. What happens in cognitive development is that when the two responses are brought into conflict, they amalgamate in some way to become higher-order rules or concepts. For example, the conflicting rules

> To find an object, search in its usual place.
> To find an object, search along its path of movement.

generate the higher-order rules

> To find an object that has not been seen to move, search in its usual place.
> To find an object that has been seen to move, search along the path of movement.

It is possible that this kind of conflict is involved in all the cognitive advances we have discussed. Consider the concept of conservation of weight. The baby can see that the object is the same object, but in a different shape. Does he tie weight to the object or does he tie weight to shape? There is conflict here, and it seems that conflict is necessary if the baby is to attain conservation of weight. Certainly, giving intensive practice to younger babies, who think that every object weighs the same, will produce a kind of pseudo-understanding of conservation, but not any actual acceleration of development. Since a baby of this age does not associate weight with length, width, or anything else, there is no possibility of conflict, and therefore no true understanding of the problem.

Conflict may also be involved in the development of skills in handling a cup. When drinking, the baby can focus on either the height of the container or the width of the container. Only if he focuses on both, however, which inevitably means some kind of conflict, does he seem able to make the requisite leap forward. In the case of determining relative size, the nature of the conflict is obvious. If the task is to stack three objects according to size, then is the middle object identified as big or as small? The only way out of this dilemma is to develop the comparative dimension—bigger than or smaller than—which is something the baby certainly does not start with.

The cognitive skills we have been discussing are interrelated in complex ways. The most basic of them seems to be the object concept. Nonetheless, development of weight conservation, number conservation, and drinking skills can, to some extent, proceed independently of the object concept, or at least, independently of the later stages involving the movement of objects in containers, changes in relative position, and so on.

All these advances are to some extent plastic, and all can be accelerated if the right environmental experiences are provided at the right developmental stage. If the appropriate experience is too prolonged or is overemphasized, the result may be inappropriate habits which prevent the baby from successfully proceeding with the tasks of interest. If the task is presented too early, the baby will simply not have the resources to cope with it and may, in fact, retreat from the learning situation altogether. The latter is by far the most damaging. A child who has been overexperimented upon, and overexposed to too many problem situations, simply retreats from all problem situations. One can truly sympathize with babies who have been overburdened with problems they cannot cope with. The whole world is a problem for the developing baby. In our efforts to channel their development, efforts which are not malign at all, we can easily overload this admirable, but limited, problem-solving capacity.

8 Language Development in Infancy

Although infancy ends with the acquisition of language, the capacity for communication does not emerge spontaneously with the advent of speech. The ability to produce sounds and to decode the sounds of human speech are present almost from birth and seem to develop without the benefit of experience. Young babies are, in fact, capable of linguistic abilities that decrease with age. It appears that the human infant is born prepared to communicate with any language community in which he finds himself. The language he eventually develops depends on the language spoken by those with whom he learns to interact in a nonverbal framework long before language appears.

A large part of infancy is spent in preparation for the use of language. What is language? What capacity is it that the two- to three-year-old has that younger babies, true infants, do not have? A precise answer to these questions is beyond my competence. The quip that any two linguists will give you three incompatible definitions of language seems to have some truth to it.

In a sense we all know what language is, because we all use language. We produce strings of noises that have meaning for those around us who speak the same language, and we understand the strings of noises that they produce. A great deal of developmental research has focused on these two aspects of language, the *productive* and the *receptive* aspects. A great amount of time has been expended on describing the sounds that children make at various ages and stages. More recently, some ingenious methods have been used to discover what sounds babies can differentiate at various ages.

Speech Discrimination in Infants

A recent study carried out by Eimas is only one example of the fascinating things we are learning about the language capacities of very young babies.[1] Babies, in fact, are capable of making very subtle linguistic discriminations, such as between the sounds *p* and *b*. Although this discrimination might sound trivial, it is actually quite difficult, for there is not much difference between the two sounds, as Figure 8.1 shows. Many adults cannot make this distinction reliably. Adults whose first language is not English, even after becoming fluent in English, may have difficulty in differentiating these particular two sounds.

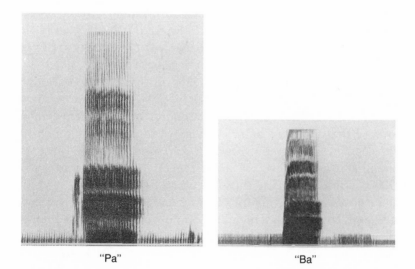

"Pa"   "Ba"

FIGURE 8.1
A spectrographic recording of the sounds *pa* and *ba*. There is little discernible difference between the *p* and *b* sounds. (From Speech and Communication Laboratory, University of Edinburgh.)

The experimental technique used in this case was a most ingenious variant of the habituation method. Two groups of four-week-old babies were given pacifiers to suck on. The pacifiers were connected up in such a way that hard sucks would switch on a loudspeaker. The loudspeaker played a *pa-pa-pa* noise to one group of babies and a *ba-ba-ba* noise to the other. At first this noise was quite interesting to the babies; they gave vigorous sucks at a fast enough rate to keep the sound on continuously. However, as we would expect, the rate of vigorous sucking declined quite rapidly.

At this point the experimenters changed things around so that the babies who had been hearing the *ba-ba-ba* sound could now hear *pa-pa-pa* instead, and vice-versa. The reasoning was that if the babies could hear this new sound as a new sound, their interest would be reawakened and vigorous sucking would begin again. This is just what happened. The new sound produced a high rate of sucking, high enough that the babies, at first, at least, could hear the noise continuously.

It seems clear that the infants in this experiment could make the very subtle distinction between the sounds *p* and *b*. The same technique has recently been used to show that Japanese babies can discriminate the sounds *l* and *r*, as in the words *fly* and *fry*. This discrimination, easily made by Japanese babies, is virtually impossible for Japanese adults.

The most striking experiment on speech perception in babies in the one described in Chapter 2 in connection with the social capacities of newborns. Condon and Sander demonstrated that newborn babies will move in precise rhythm with the segments of human speech, a response they called interactional synchrony.[2] In fact, adult speech is a pretty continuous flow of stimulation, and the units are marked by very tiny variations in stimulation (Figure 8.2). As adults we usually experience a foreign language as a meaningless flow of sound. If the linguistic base is different from that of our native tongue, we are hard put to pick out words, much less the units that make up words. Young babies suffer no such limitation. Remember that the babies in this study showed interactional synchrony whether they were addressed in English or in Chinese. In other words,

Then the North   Wind   blew   as   hard   as   he   could

FIGURE 8.2

The flow of sound in a sentence. (From Speech and Communication Laboratory, University of Edinburgh.)

they could pick out the units of Chinese speech, something the adults around them would not be able to do.

This is a truly astonishing feat. It substantiates a hypothesis put forward by many people that babies are born ready to take their place in any language community, ready to make any speech discriminations that this community demands of them.

Vocalization in Infancy

The same hypothesis has been offered in connection with the vocal productions of young babies. Vocalizing has two distinct developmental phases. During their first six months, babies develop a repertoire of vocalizations which is astounding. It has been claimed that the repertoire of the babbling baby in the first half-year contains all the sounds of all the languages of man. This vast repertoire does not persist. By the second half-year of life the baby is producing pretty much only the sounds of the language community in which he finds himself. If the language of the adults around him is English, he produces the sounds that characterize English. If they speak French, he produces the sounds of French. If they speak Russian, he produces the sounds of Russian, and so on. It seems that the baby retains in his repertoire only those sounds that he hears from others in his environment.[3]

It is truly amazing that young babies produce with such fluency sounds which are completely beyond us as adults struggling to learn a second language. It is small consolation to know that as infants we made all the noises we have such difficulty producing now. It seems the baby comes into the world ready to participate in all possible linguistic communities. Apparently he is able to produce the sounds of any language while he is small. Then, with increasing age, the range of sounds he can articulate gradually becomes limited to the sounds produced by the adults around him. It seems plausible that the range of sounds he can distinguish is similarly restricted.

Restriction of this sort may seem a regrettable loss. However, this restriction serves an important function since our information-handling capacity is limited. In general, the ease with which we pick up or detect a stimulus depends more on the number of stimuli that might occur than on the characteristics of that particular stimulus. Similarly, the speed and ease with which we can make a response depends on the number of responses we might have to make, rather than on the characteristics of that response. By restricting the range of sounds he is prepared to hear, the baby becomes able to process those he does attend to with greater ease. He is able to pay more attention to sound sequences, the chains of sounds that make up the words of a particular language. Similarly, by cutting down on the range of sounds he produces, he becomes better able to integrate these sounds to produce words.

The Processes Underlying
Language Development

We do not have a clear understanding of the developmental processes by which the baby changes from a state of being ready for any language to the point of producing the words of a specific language. We do know that the experience of hearing language is necessary for this transformation to occur. The consequences of not hearing language may be a permanent infancy. In some mysterious way, the developing child gradually loses the capacity to acquire language. The reason for this loss is simply not known at present.

It is commonly claimed that the experience of hearing a spoken language is enough to ensure that a child will come to speak that language. The language heard, apparently, need not be embedded in any kind of reward context. The late Eric Lenneberg maintained that the sound of a radio tuned to a talk show was a sufficient stimulus for normal linguistic development.[4] He based this conclusion on studies of the children of deaf-mute parents. The parents could not talk to one another or to their child. The children nonetheless developed language skills at a normal rate in the normal way, provided there was some source of speech input around them, even one as unresponsive as a radio.

While explanations such as Lenneberg's may hold for the productive and receptive aspects of language, I must confess that I am dubious about their validity as an account of the development of language as a system of communication. The noise-making aspects of language have preoccupied psychologists to such an extent that, until recently, the development of communication was totally ignored. This is a deplorable oversight, for the essence of language is not noise, but communication, and obviously, communication is possible without words. The newborn baby communicates. By engaging in synchronic interaction with adults, the baby is communicating something—that he is one of us, for example, that he is with us. Interpersonal communion of this kind can also be conveyed in words, but it need not be. "Togetherness" seems to be the main message communicated in the nonverbal exchanges described in Chapter 4. The linguist Halliday refers to this as the *interpersonal* function of language. For Halliday there are seven basic functions in language:

1. The *instrumental* function is the function that language serves of satisfying the child's material needs, of enabling him to obtain the goods and services that he

wants. This is the "I want" function of language; and it is likely to include a general expression of desire, some element meaning simply "I want that object there (present in the context)," as well as perhaps other expressions relating to specific desires, responses to questions "Do you want. . . ?" and so on.

2. The *regulatory* function is related to this, but it is also distinct. It is the function of language as controlling the behaviour of others, something which the child recognizes very easily because language is used on him in this way: language is used to control his own behaviour and he soon learns that he can turn the tables and use it to control others. The regulatory is the "do as I tell you" function of language. The difference between this and the instrumental is that in the instrumental the focus is on the goods or services required and it does not matter who provides them, whereas regulatory utterances are directed towards a particular individual, and it is the behaviour of that individual that is to be influenced. Typically therefore this function includes meanings such as, again, a generalized request "Do that" meaning "Do what you have just been doing (in the context)," "Do that again": as well as various specific demands, particularly in the form of suggestions "Let's do . . . ," such as "Let's go for a walk," "Let's play this game," "Let's sing a song" and so forth.

3. The *interpersonal* function is what we might gloss as the "me and you" function of language. This is language used by the child to interact with those around him, particularly his mother and others that are important to him, and it includes meanings such as generalized greetings "Hello," "Pleased to see you", and also responses to calls "Yes?," as well as more specific forms. For example, the first names of particular individuals that the child learns are typically used with a purely interactional function; and there may be other specific meanings of an interactional kind involving the focussing of attention on particular objects in the environment, some favourite objects of the child which are used as channels for interacting with those around him. . . ."

4. Fourthly there is the *personal* function. This is language used to express the child's own uniqueness; to express his awareness of himself, in contradistinction to his envi-

ronment, and then to mould that self—ultimately, language in the development of the personality. This includes, therefore, expressions of personal feelings, of participation and withdrawal, of interest, pleasure, disgust, and so forth, and extends later on to more specific intrusion of the child as a personality into the speech situation. We might call this the "here I come" function of language.

5.   Fifthly, once the boundary between the child himself and his environment is beginning to be recognised, then the child can turn towards the exploration of the environment; this is the *heuristic* function of language, the "tell me why" function, that which later on develops into the whole range of questioning forms that the young child uses. At this very early stage, in its most elementary form the heuristic use of language is the demand for a name, which is the child's way of categorizing the objects of the physical world; but it soon expands into a variety of more specific meanings.

6.   Finally we have the *imaginative* function, which is the function of language whereby the child creates an environment of his own. As well as moving into, taking over and exploring the universe which he finds around him, the child also uses language for creating a universe of his own, a world initially of pure sound, but which gradually turns into one of story and make-believe and let's pretend, and ultimately into the realm of poetry and imaginative writing. This we may call the "let's pretend" function of language.

There is in fact a seventh to be added to the list; . . . this is the one that we can call the *informative* function of language, the "I've got something to tell you" function. . . .[5]

Halliday has described the development of one child's ability to use these functions. At ten-and-a-half months his subject had the language repertoire shown in Table 8.1. This is really a very large repertoire. Note that very little of it bears any relation to the sounds made by adults. The meaning of the sounds the baby makes must be inferred from gestures and context. According to Halliday, this is not especially difficult. Certainly parents seem able to work out what their baby wants with a fairly high success rate, although strangers do not seem to cope anything like so well.

TABLE 8.1
The Language Repertoire of a Baby at 10½ Months*

Function	Content Systems	Expression (Articulation)	Approximate Sound	Meaning
Instrumental →	demand, general	nã - - -	nyah (repeat)	give me that
	demand, specific (toy bird)	bø	bih (as in bird)	give me my bird
Regulatory →	command, normal	ə̃	nyih	do that (again)
	command, intensified	m̃ŋ̂	mnying!	do that right now!
Interactional →	initiation → normal (friendly)	= ø; ðø; ðo	ih; dih; doh (as in doll)	nice to see you (& shall we look at this together?)
	initiation → intensified (impatient)	ə̃nːnː	ihngIngIng	nice to see you—at last!
	response	ɛ; ə	eh (as in yes); ih	yes it's me
Personal →	participation → interest → general	= ø	ih	that's interesting
	participation → interest → specific (movement)	ðø; bø; ø	do (as in dot); bih; ih	look it's moving (? a dog, birds)
	participation → pleasure → general	a	ah	that's nice
	participation → pleasure → specific (taste)	n̂ŋ	nying	that tastes nice
	withdrawal	ġʷɤ̃ː - - -	(gurgle)	I'm sleepy

*The sounds cannot be accurately described except by using phonetic notation, shown in the Expression column. The entries under Approximate Sound are very approximate indeed. At 0; 9, Nigel had two meanings, both expressed as [ø] on mid or mid-low falling tone; one interactional, "let's be together", the other (usually with the wider interval) personal, "look, it's moving". He also had another three meanings expressed gesturally: two instrumental, "I want that", grasping object firmly, and "I don't want that", touching object lightly; and one regulatory, "do that again", touching person or relevant object firmly (e.g. "making that jump in the air again"). The gestures disappeared during NL 1-2.
SOURCE: After Halliday, 1975.

The Development
of Communication Skills

Halliday did not carry out (or at least has not published) a systematic study of the development that went on before the stage he describes. Although the newborn cannot communicate as extensively as the ten-month-old, newborns do communicate. They communicate togetherness, the interpersonal function, in their synchronous response to human speech. Crying, which newborns certainly can do, might seem to be a clear instance of the instrumental function. However, very careful observational studies indicate that early crying is a response to discomfort rather than the request for attention it later becomes. Wolff places the onset of the latter kind of crying in the third week of life. Rather unkindly, he calls it "fake crying," describing this cry as

> . . . of a low pitch and intensity; it consists of long drawn out moans which occasionally rise to more explicit cries, and then revert to poorly articulated moans. A mother will respond to the fake cry in one of various ways which largely depend on her general style and momentary disposition. More often than not she ignores such sounds until they become full-fledged rhythmical cries; at other times she picks the baby up to comfort him, or else changes his position so that he can see her while she works.[6]

Wolff also makes the interesting observation that noncrying vocalization appears at about the same time as these fake cries and in the same context, seemingly functioning as calls for attention, perhaps subserving the instrumental and personal functions simultaneously.

By the eighth week babies are using sounds for the personal and the interpersonal function. Wolff describes the behavior thus:

> The baby's non-cry vocalizations diversify rapidly between the sixth and eighth week, and now novel sounds are no longer discovered in a context of fussiness. The baby invents new noises while he is playing alone, including "Bronx cheers," gurgling, and tongue games and then practices them in circular fashion. On the sound spectrogram these sounds are more complex, and to the ear the individual types of vocalizations are more discreet.

Exercise of new vocalizations is more prolific when the baby is not distracted by persons moving about in the room, so that the best recordings of novel sounds are obtained from behind a screen. The baby's private conversations can be interrupted by silent visual contact; at the same time one can initiate 'conversation' with the baby by imitating his vocalizations and encouraging him to talk even when he was previously silent. I have tested this effect by alternately nodding my head *silently* for five minutes, then *babbling* and nodding for five minutes, then nodding silently for another five minutes, etc., recording the session, and comparing the amount of baby vocalizations under the two conditions (whole sequence can be reversed systematically). In this way it is possible to demonstrate a significantly greater amount of vocalizations when the partner talks than when he is silent. A spectrographic comparison of the sounds made by the experimenter and the baby show that an adult cannot in any strict sense imitate the baby's voice pattern, and that baby vocalizations are not direct copies of the sounds adults made (see Lenneberg, 1964). But once the baby has several discreet sounds at his disposal which he has practiced in circular fashion, one can demonstrate that the infant makes some effort to imitate the sounds he hears. When the observer, for example, introduces low-pitched *da-da* sounds which are a part of the infant's repertory, while the infant is making high-pitched squeals, the baby stops squealing and produces his own version of the low-pitched *da-da* sounds. When the observer then imitates the earlier high-pitched squeals the infant resumes his own version of squealing. Even at this stage it seems legitimate within limits, to speak of vocal imitations, not in the sense of direct copies, but as an active "accommodation" of vocal patterns which are already at the infant's disposal; the baby acts as if the adult's sound was sufficiently like his own to make him want to "perpetuate" what he has heard.[7]

Some time after the fourth month the pointing gesture is added to the baby's repertoire. This gesture is designed to attract the attention of another person to an object or event of interest. If a four-month-old baby is shown a desirable toy that is out of reach, the baby will typically do nothing. An older baby will extend his hand toward the object. This hand gesture is different from reaching; the hand is quite limp, and there is no finger-thumb opposition for grasping (Figure 8.3). The extension

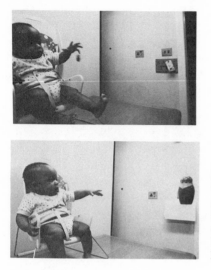

FIGURE 8.3
Whereas a baby will reach for and grasp an object that is within reach, the gesture toward an object that is clearly out of range *(below)* looks more like pointing. (Photos by T. G. R. Bower.)

of the hand is often accompanied by "gimme" noises. It is, in fact, a form of pointing. It may be accompanied by "what's that?" noises, too, if the event is novel to the baby. Pointing may also be used to subserve interpersonal needs. Looking at things together is something that babies seem to enjoy.

It is striking that throughout this phase of development, up to the age of nine or ten months, babies are using sounds and gestures in a communicational way, but the sounds remain private to the baby. By and large, they are not the sounds used by adults. The privacy of this early language was most forcibly brought home to me by two pairs of twins. Each twin developed a "gimme" noise that would accompany pointing. However, each child had a unique noise. Not even the pair of identical twins made the same noise for the same purpose.

How does this private vocal language become shaped into the public language of the child's community? It is hard to believe that listening to a radio is enough. What seems more likely is that adults decode the meaning of the baby's utterances by looking at the specific nonverbal behaviors, nonverbal gestures, and so on that accompany them. The adults may then utter the correct sound. As a result of processes of association, the baby may come to grasp that he will be more efficient in getting the

TABLE 8.2
The Language Repertoire of the Same Baby at 18 Months*

Function	Content Systems		Expression (Articulation)	Approximate Sound	Meaning
Instrumental	demand, general	initiation — object present	? nã - - -	gnyah (repeat)	give me that
		response — service or non-visible object	yi - -	yee (repeat)	yes I want that
			a:	ahhh	yes I want what you just offered
	demand, specific	powder	bʷ ġa(-); buġ(-)	biwigah (repeat); boog (repeat)	I want some powder
		clock	tƙa(-); tƙɔ(-)	tikah (repeat); tikoh (repeat)	I want (to go and get) the clock
Regulatory	command, general	initiation — normal	a; ɜ; ɜ̃	ah; eh; nyeh	do that (again)
		intensified	m̂nŋ	mnying!	do that right now!
		response — positive	ɔ̄ - - -	nyeh (repeat)	yes (/let's) do that
		negative	ãã	nyahnyah	no don't (/let's) do that
	command, specific	go for walk	' - - -	—	let's go for a walk
		play with cat	pʷi - - -; peʷ	pwee (repeat)	let me play with the cat

Interactional / Personal / Imaginative system network (after Halliday, 1975):

Function	Expression	Approximate Sound	Gloss
Interactional — greeting, personalized — Anna	na; an; a	nan!; ann-an!	Anna!
Interactional — greeting, personalized — Daddy	da; dada	dah!; dahdah!	Daddy!
engagement — response — to interaction	ʔɛ˞ :	eh	yes it's me; yes, I see
engagement — response — to regulation (reproof)	ø	ih	don't be cross with me
engagement — initiation — object-oriented — normal	*a::da	ahh-dah	look, a picture; you say what it is
engagement — initiation — object-oriented — subsequent	a::da	ahh-dahh	another picture; now say what that one is
engagement — initiation — person-oriented	=₁æ(dæ--) dæ; ɛ(dɛ--) dɛ	aahdaah; ehdeh	nice to see you ((& shall we look at this?))
Personal — participation — interest — general	=₁æ(dæ--) dæ	aahdaah	look, that's interesting
Personal — participation — interest — specific — dog	da	dah!	a dog!
Personal — participation — interest — specific — bird	ba	bah!	birds!
Personal — participation — interest — specific — bus	ba	bah!	a bus!
Personal — participation — interest — specific — aeroplane	œɯœ	ihhih!	an aeroplane!
Personal — participation — pleasure	ɛ˞i:; æ˞i:	ehyee; ahyee	that's nice
Personal — participation — surprise	m̃n̩n̩	mnying!	that's funny (look where it's gone!)
Personal — participation — disgust	bʷ ġa(-); buġˀ(-) ---	biwigah (repeat); boog (repeat)	a lot of talk!
Personal — withdrawal	=₂ ġʷˠɩ --- =₂	(gurgle)	I'm sleepy
Imaginative — pretend-play			let's pretend to go to sleep
Imaginative — song	bʷɜ ---	bwiheh	tra-la-la

*The sounds cannot be accurately described except by using phonetic notation, shown in the Expression column. The entries under Approximate Sound are very approximate indeed.
SOURCE: After Halliday, 1975.

145

things he wants if he uses the sounds or words that adults already use. Halliday relates one instance of a child trying, as he puts it, very patiently to explain what a particular noise meant. The child repeated the noise slowly and carefully with a wealth of gestures, and so on, but his father simply could not understand what the child wanted. This sound apparently dropped out of the baby's repertoire pretty much instantaneously.

It seems possible that reinforcement processes of this sort are necessary for the child to come to use the sounds used by adults. Babies in institutions, it is often claimed, will develop language interactions with one another that are incomprehensible to adults. They are commonly described as babbling nonsensically to one another and laughing all the while. "Babbling nonsensically" may be a harsh way to put it. The sounds that the babies utter may have meaning for them within a code system that they have developed. In an institutional environment there is less opportunity for language development to be reinforced and directed by adults, and correspondingly more opportunity for the babies to develop a private crib language to share with their neighbors. There are certainly a great number of reports of twins developing private languages which they do not share with their parents. Apparently the emergence of comprehensible sounds depends on some shaping by cooperative adults.

The kind of change that goes on is illustrated in Table 8.2, which shows the range of vocalizations that Halliday's subject could produce at eighteen months. Note that the sounds are recognizable English now. Obviously a great advance has been made since the stage recorded in Table 8.1. However, this advance has still not taken the baby into language proper. At this age the sounds are still situationally specific. Words which would be appropriate in many situations are still used only in the context in which they were learned. This baby, for example, used *more* only in the context of getting more cereal, although it would have been appropriate elsewhere. The commands or requests were tied to a specific stimulus situation.

Language proper begins when the "words" in the vocabulary can be used in any situation. In a sense, this development is not limited to language. The child is using his responses in new situations throughout infancy. Possibly success in using established responses in new situations facilitates the generalization of utterances to all possible situations. This is something on which there are no data, something, indeed, on which it would be hard to gather data. The important point, however, is that all during infancy the baby is preparing in all ways to stop being an infant, to begin using language. Once he has reached this stage, he has stepped beyond the confines of this book and is no longer an infant.

9 The Long-Term Effects of Infancy

The question that has long plagued psychologists and parents alike is the extent to which experiences in infancy–and particularly the lack of those experiences which are normal to infancy–are the determining factors for subsequent personality and cognitive development. Although the long-term effects of experiences in infancy are to some extent reversible in the case of personality, on the whole, the foundations that are laid in this period of life seem to remain fairly stable. In the case of cognitive development the patterns established in infancy seem not to be reversible. The reason for this difference is that total deprivation of certain key experiences is possible for cognitive development, but is not possible for personality development.

Throughout the last eight chapters we have looked at the process of development in infancy. A fascinating process it is, but how significant is this segment of development? Does the development that goes on at this stage of life program all subsequent development, or is infancy merely a passing phase, giving way to more potent developmental influences after the onset of language? What we are asking here is whether experiences in infancy have long-term effects on the individual. This is a question that has attracted great interest for many years.

The extreme nativist, of course, would argue that experiences in infancy have no special importance because all human development is essentially the result of gene expression. We have considered sufficient data, in my opinion, to discount the

extreme nativist position on development in infancy, and therefore, by extension, in the longer term too. Recall, for example,
that identical twins who looked different, and were therefore
treated differently, were found to develop different temperaments and responses to the world around them.[1] According to
nativist theory, these babies should develop identically since
they have identical genes. The nativist account of personality
development, at least, must therefore be ruled out.

Further evidence of the role of early experience is the effect
of blindness on motor development. Deprived of the specific
inputs from the environment available to the sighted child, the
motor development of blind babies can take very bizarre turns.
Finally, as we saw in Chapter 7, specific inputs are required to
trigger certain cognitive advances. It seems clear, then, that
specific inputs from the environment do affect the course of
development in infancy.

Nevertheless, the idea that infancy is a relatively unimportant stage seems to prevail among many of those involved in
setting up compensatory-education programs, such as Head
Start. The underlying assumption has been that special educational experiences beginning at three years of age or so would be
sufficient to compensate for deprivations suffered prior to that
time. This assumption also seems to have been proved wrong.

Does this mean that infancy is a critical period for development, with long-term consequences for all subsequent
stages? The issue here is really one of *reversibility*. Can the effects
of a poor environment in infancy be reversed in later life by a
good environment? Can the effects of a good environment in
infancy be reversed by a bad environment in later life? Let us
consider the evidence on these issues.

Maternal Deprivation
and Personality Development

There has been great popular interest in the consequences
of any disruption in the affectional attachments a child forms
during infancy. Beginning about 1950, numerous authoritative
figures, representing such prestigious bodies as the World

Health Organization, began warning all the world that any deviation from the normal Western pattern of mothering, the pattern leading to the all-important infant-mother attachment, could cause irreparable damage to the developing child. Deviations from the Western norm were labeled maternal deprivation. Maternal deprivation was alleged to be the cause of criminal behavior, psychopathic behavior, and a whole slew of other behavioral disturbances. The search for maternal deprivation at times became a witchhunt, with otherwise sensible people going so far as to claim that when a mother read a book in the presence of her child, she was in some sense depriving the child of his or her due share of maternal care and attention.[2]

In recent years the demand for women in the workforce has meant that many mothers have been unable to meet these demands for full-time maternal care of every baby (Figure 9.1). Many have felt themselves to be depriving mothers, and have felt guilt over what they saw as their infliction of maternal deprivation on their own children. Still others have contended that this argument was merely a male chauvinist plot to keep women safely relegated to the kitchen.

What is the most reasonable position in this ideologically overloaded controversy? The data that gave rise to the maternal-deprivation dogma were derived from retrospective studies, mostly of delinquent boys. In studying these boys to try to find out why they had become delinquent, it turned out that a significant proportion of them had either had no consistent attachment figure in early infancy, or else had lost that attachment figure owing to death, divorce, or whatever. Some of these boys apparently were a particularly terrifying form of psycho-

FIGURE 9.1
Child-care arrangements for working mothers often include private homes, in which a "babysitter," who may have young babies of her own, cares for a limited number of children on a regular basis. (From The Scotsman Publications Ltd. Used by permission.)

path, the *affectionless character*. The affectionless character is described as someone superficially charming, easily forming friendships, skilled in manipulating people, who nonetheless feels no human emotions, no warmth, no generosity, no love at all. As painted, the affectionless character is a terrifying, heartless monster indeed, and all because of maternal deprivation.

The theorizing about maternal deprivation was given a tremendous boost by advances in ethology, especially those concerning the phenomenon of imprinting. Imprinting appears to be a genetically stereotyped sequence of behavior most typical of birds that can walk as soon as they leave the egg. Such birds will characteristically follow the first moving thing they see after hatching. In most cases the first moving thing they see after hatching is their biological mother. In some cases, however, the first thing the birds saw was a large, bearded ethologist. When he started to move, they followed him. If they were later presented with their biological mother, they ignored her and continued to follow their substitute mother. If the ethologist left, the baby birds showed typical separation anxiety. They would run around chirping anxiously until reunited with him and would accept no substitute. In some cases, in adult life, birds who had imprinted on an adult human were unable to relate to their own species and would attempt to mate only with humans.[3]

Some birds were isolated after hatching, so that there was no opportunity for them to imprint. It was found in such cases that after a *critical period* these baby birds would follow nothing and no one. For the rest of their lives they were social isolates. Even adult sex drives could not lead them into social interaction with other members of their species, or indeed with anything at all.

The pressure to draw conclusions from these results about the human case was greatly increased by Harlow's discovery of artificial attachments in rhesus monkeys, an animal much closer to the human case than the birds from whom the data had been initially drawn. What Harlow did was to raise rhesus monkeys in complete isolation from one another and from any animate, real, live monkey mother.[4] The babies survived until adulthood quite well. When adult, they were, however, completely deviant. They would not interact with other adults at all, not even for sexual purposes. Those few females who were impregnated by and large ignored or killed their babies.

The stage was thus set for an extension of these findings along the following lines. There is a critical period in human development within which a baby must form an attachment to a single human adult. For this attachment to be formed, the baby must have a one-to-one relationship with a single human caretaker, preferably, but not necessarily, his biological mother. That relationship will provide him with a model for all his subsequent relationships in life. Any child who fails to form this crucial attachment in infancy will forever remain incapable of forming relationships and will become that chilling apparition, the affectionless character. If that child is a girl, and she reproduces, there will be a growing population of affectionless characters in the world. And that would be the way the world ended.

The problems supposedly stemming from maternal deprivation have been put down to two factors. One is the lack of a model to serve as the basis for relationships with others. This applies only if there has been no opportunity to develop attachments. However, if attachments have been made and then broken, a different pathology is supposed to develop. The mother figure is supposed to signify relief from all need. Thus her absence in some way comes to be a signal for anxiety, a lasting anxiety if the separation is permanent.

Of these two different pathologies, it is the former which has caused the greatest popular furor. Working mothers of young children are exposed to a certain amount of public censure. Women who work will include the fear of being depriving mothers among their many reasons for choosing not to have children.

In many respects, the whole issue seems to have been greatly exaggerated. The original cause for concern was the seemingly high proportion of individuals with nonnormal mothering in their backgrounds who came to the attention of the authorities or the mental-health profession. These initial studies were *retrospective*. The investigators had a defined population of abnormal individuals, and the backgrounds of those individuals were scanned for possible reasons for their abnormality. Studies of this kind are a fertile source of hypotheses about the causes of any particular state. However, while retrospective data may generate a hypothesis, they can never be used to establish or test it. Prospective studies are required to test any hypothesis.

What does this mean in the maternal-deprivation case? It means that we must find a population of individuals who never had the opportunity to form an attachment to one individual during the critical period. We must then establish a control group of children matched for sex, age, nutritional circumstances, educational opportunity, and so on, who did have an opportunity to form such an attachment. Then we must compare the two groups. Any difference between them, if we have done the matching properly, will be due to the effects of having or not having an attachment figure during infancy. According to the maternal-deprivation hypothesis, the nonattached group should be significantly more likely to become criminal, antisocial, or mentally ill. Such studies have been done.[5] In none of these studies has there been any very significant difference between the two groups.

The clinical picture of the effects of maternal deprivation and separation from the mother is thus far from clear. It seems that substitute mothering, where someone else looks after the baby while the mother works, has no adverse effects on development. Indeed, some findings indicate that this kind of situation can be good for babies (Figure 9.2). The same thing seems

FIGURE 9.2
Recent studies indicate that close communication between father and infant is an important factor in personality development for girls as well as boys. (Photo by Nancy R. Tenney.)

to be true of day care. Day care was roundly condemned in the 1950s. More recent work indicates that it has no adverse effects on either cognitive or social development, and may, in fact, have clearly good effects.

The situation with the worst consequences is the one in which the baby is left alone, attended only by an ever-changing succession of caretakers. This is the situation originally claimed to produce the affectionless character. Under these circumstances there is no opportunity for the child to develop anything other than a surface range of communication skills. As we saw in Chapter 4, even these children can catch up and develop quite normal intense relationships. Some, of course, do not.

I tend to think that the way we label a particular affectionless child may be what determines whether or not that child can outgrow the state. If we encounter a three-year-old who has never had a chance to develop deep communication skills, we are meeting someone who really only has the skills of an average six-month-old. If we treat him like a six-month-old in this one respect, some progress may be possible. If, however, the child is labeled as a deviant or bad three-year-old, then progress is probably impossible. We are asking the child to demonstrate skills he simply does not have. If we do not help him develop them, there is no way he can do it for himself. At some point development may become impossible, but that point is quite late for the communication skills that make up personality.

In fairness to the maternal-deprivation theory, it should be said that such studies have always found some disadvantaged children among the maternally deprived groups. However, the disadvantage is far from universal. In fact, the most notable characteristic is the way children are able to thrive in what seem to be conditions of severe maternal deprivation. The case of the refugee children described in Chapter 4 is a striking example.[6] These children, raised in terror by an ever-changing group of adults, adults on their way to a foreknown death, had developed attachments—to one another. As pointed out earlier, the fact that these children had formed attachments to one another is a death blow to one version of maternal-deprivation theory.

The fact of the attachments, of course, means that these children, although maternally deprived, were not attachment deprived. Is it possible that it is attachment deprivation, rather than maternal deprivation, that is important? Is it, as Harlow's work with monkeys seems to suggest, the attachment itself that is important, rather than attachment to a specific adult, whether mother or mother substitute?

At this point some clarification of terms is needed. We must ask to what extent attachment deprivation is possible. As we saw in Chapter 4, in the case of human infants, attachment is actually the construction of a rich set of communicational routines involving specific meanings and specific interchanges. These interchanges are nonverbal, and the meaning units are arbitrary and specific to the particular communicating pair. They are not like words or sentences, which have the same meaning (more or less) between any communicating pair.

If there is no one with whom the child can develop this rich nonverbal framework, as must be obvious, he cannot develop it. Schaffer showed, in fact, that development simply does not occur under those circumstances.[7] What of a child with multiple, ever-changing caretakers, all of whom do interact with him or her? Such children will develop a wide range of communication skills that do not go very deep. They are commonly described as facile, charming, and shallow. What else could they be?

Is there any reason to believe that these handicaps in development need be permanent? In other words, can they be reversed? The large-scale prospective studies described by Rutter have shown that they can be.[8] We also know from the more detailed studies by Schaffer that children, babies, will very rapidly pick up the communication skills appropriate to their age. Is there any time limit on this process of catching up? There probably is, but it is very late. Even the various wild children who have been described—such as Genie, who was twelve years old before being introduced to the possibilities of communication—still seemed able to catch up to some considerable extent.[9] In any kind of normal environment, even the environment of an impersonal institution, the children, once they are sufficiently mobile, can communicate with one another, form attachments to one another.

What of the normal home situation? Does a mother stand a chance of losing her child's attachment if she surrenders a part of the caretaking process to someone else? It must be pointed out that 100 percent care is no guarantee of exclusive attachment. Recall that 20 percent of the babies in Schaffer's study formed their first attachments to someone who took no part in their care at all, someone whose sole link was in communicational behavior. Second, we must question the necessity, or indeed the normality, in statistical terms, of the one-to-one attachment idealized by maternal-deprivation theorists. Nearly one-third of the babies in Schaffer's study showed multiple attachments right from the start. This was in Scotland, where one-to-one care patterns predominate. Around the world many-to-one patterns are more common and do not seem to have the disasterous effects posited by early versions of maternal-deprivation theory. There seems little empirical basis for the claim that an exclusive one-to-one attachment is necessary for the well-being of the child. Indeed, in a world where children are in short supply, a world of zero population growth, the well-being of adults might demand multiple attachments of the few babies around.

Note that I am not saying that the absence of normal opportunities to form attachments is a good thing. It is quite clear that it is a bad thing. However, the bulk of the evidence seems to indicate that the effects of temporary deprivation can be reversed.

What of the good effects of normal attachment formation? Can these be reversed if the child is later placed in a "bad" environment? This can happen, for example, if a child loses his parents and then must be placed in institutional care. There are two influences at work here. One is the actual loss of attachment figures. The other is the effect of the institutional environment itself. It seems that children who have had a good social environment in infancy are well buffered against both these malign influences and show little, if any, impairment in later social or intellectual functioning. Statistically, the outcome is somewhat less happy if the cause of separation is divorce. It is speculated that the factors causing such a breakup in the first place may be the very ones that deprive the baby of an opportunity for communicational interaction with the adults around him. Again, it must be emphasized that the adverse effects of divorce are far from universal. In fact, in view of the large number of children raised by divorced parents, they are obviously the exception rather than the rule.

What can we say, then, about the effects of maternal-care patterns on personality development? Good maternal care in infancy, care which allows the development of deep and intimate communicational routines, seems to produce *irreversible* good effects on the developing child. The lack of this kind of care produces bad effects, but effects which are *reversible*, however difficult the process may be. The difficulty of reversing bad effects and the robustness of the good effects incline me at least to assert that infancy is indeed the most important segment of life for developing those interpersonal skills we call personality. A happy baby is most likely to become a happy adult.

Sex Identity

One aspect of personality that seems to remain relatively stable after infancy is sex identity. The evidence for this proposition comes from studies of individuals whose gender was mislabeled at birth and then relabeled when it was found the baby had been assigned the wrong sex. If the switch is made early in infancy, sometimes with the help of corrective surgery, no long-term ill effects are found. However, it is much more difficult to enforce a change after infancy is over. Money gives three years as the absolute upper limit.[10] Beyond that time, it seems to be impossible to unlearn how to be a boy and to learn how to be a girl, and vice versa.

The Effect of Feeding Schedules on Personality

Scientists have searched hard for other long-term consequences of treatment in infancy on later personality. One favored research area has been the effect of feeding schedules on later personality. Feeding schedules can vary from a completely ad lib basis, where the baby is simply fed whenever he demands food, to completely programmed feeding, where the baby is fed according to a rigid schedule, even if this means waking him to feed him. In theory, these two extremes should have different effects on development. An analogous case is the development of blind babies, where the lack of opportunity to initiate and control action seems to lead to generalized passivity. It seems plausible that the enforced passivity of a rigid, preprogrammed feeding schedule should be an especially potent way of promoting generalized passivity and dependency.

The research that has been done in this area supports the idea that preprogrammed feeding does promote passive dependency.[11] However, the effect is short lived. It is noticeable at the age of entry to nursery school, but not at the age of entry to grade school. Just why this is so is not known. It seems possible that once the child is mobile, and particularly once the child mixes with other children, new habits of action can be acquired, overcoming those laid down in infancy.

At the most basic levels of personality formation, experience in infancy does thus seem to be critical. The formation of skills in interacting with people is easy in infancy and becomes increasingly difficult thereafter. The assumption of a gender identity also seems to occur in infancy, and to be irreversible thereafter. More subtle aspects of personality are shaped in infancy, too, but these seem to be more plastic. Once the child is mobile, once the child can talk, apparently some patterns of behavior can be modified. Despite this, I would still assert that infancy is the most significant period of life for personality formation.

Long-Term Consequences
of Visual Restriction

Although experiences in infancy are not the sole determinants of personality development, certain experiences do seem to be critical for other aspects of development. One slightly surprising (to me at least) set of results bears on the effects of restriction of visual experience on visual development. The visual system is well-formed at birth. Some babies are born with cataracts that prevent them from using this visual system. These cataracts can be removed (Figure 9.3). However, it appears that unless the operation is done very early in infancy, the whole enterprise is not worthwhile. Even the neural structures present at birth will disappear if they are not used during the first months of life. Once this has happened, it seems that it is difficult, if not impossible, to restore them.

The structures mediating binocular vision are even more sensitive. As described in Chapter 5, binocular vision is a perceptual capacity that is affected by growth. Before it can be useful, it must be calibrated. Even one week of restriction to monocular vision, owing to an eye infection, for example, can apparently limit the possibility of firm establishment of binocular vision. The precise period of sensitivity is not known, but it appears to be at its greatest in the first six months of life and is definitely over by the age of eighteen months.

Binocular vision seems to be the most delicate of all human perceptual functions, the one most sensitive to upset. However, the upset—restriction to monocularity—must occur during infancy to have any permanent effect. After that time, there is

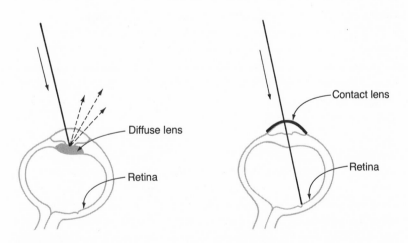

FIGURE 9.3
With cataract, the lens of the eye diffuses light rays, so that no patterned light reaches the retina to form an image. This condition can be corrected surgically, with a contact lens implanted to serve the function of the normal lens.

little effect even of a prolonged period of monocular vision. Once the system is fixed, by experience during infancy, it is apparently robust enough to withstand later assaults.[12]

Something similar, though ultimately more mysterious, seems to occur in cognitive development. The baby develops a very sophisticated set of concepts during the course of infancy. This development is sufficiently robust to withstand even such grave handicaps as the lack of limbs, and consequent complete loss of manipulative experience, as in the case of thalidomide babies. Nonetheless, there are handicaps against which conceptual development is not completely buffered. Blindness is the most striking instance of this.

Congenital blindness interferes with motor development, as we saw in Chapter 6. It also interferes with conceptual development in a variety of ways. In Chapter 7 we discussed the process by which the baby acquires an understanding of the possible spatial relationships between objects, relationships such as *on, in, behind,* and *in front* and *between.* Obviously, success with problems like the one outlined in Figure 7.7 depends on comprehension and integration of concepts such as "on the right," "in the middle," "on the left," as well as distance relationships. These relationships are specified in vision, although their integration requires more central processes.

The sighted child solves these problems by the age of eighteen months. There is some evidence that congenitally blind children never solve them. The congenitally blind child apparently never acquires a spatial framework for judgments about the relative position of objects.[13] The spontaneous framework he uses instead is a temporal one.

This was quite clearly brought out in an ingenious experiment by O'Connor and Hermelin.[14] Three loudspeakers, set up as shown in Figure 9.4, emitted three different sounds—say, "five," "seven," "nine"—and the child was asked which number came in the middle. Regardless of which digit came from the middle loudspeaker, the blind children invariably chose the temporal middle, ignoring the possible spatial-ordering rule.

A similar reliance on temporal ordering seems to underlie the difficulties the blind child has with a problem like the one in Figure 9.5. The answer most commonly given by blind children

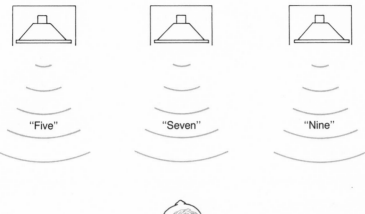

FIGURE 9.4
If sounds are emitted by the loudspeakers in the sequence "five, seven, nine" or "nine, seven, five," their temporal order follows the spatial order of the sound sources (left to right or right to left). With the sequence "seven, nine, five" or "nine, five, seven," the temporal order violates the spatial order; the number in the temporal middle is not emitted by the middle loudspeaker. In this situation blind children will ignore the possibility of spatial order altogether and invariably identify the "middle number" as the one in the temporal middle.

to the question of which thing will reach a particular station first depends on the order in which they touch the objects. Sighted infants can solve such problems at a behavioral level before the end of infancy. Blind children cannot solve them at all.

The most striking evidence of the incapacities of blind children is a study by Drever of a number of highly intelligent, congenitally blind children who had actually succeeded in passing university entrance examinations in Euclidean geometry.[15] They had done so by memorization of Euclid's theorems. They had no understanding of these theorems at all and could not solve the simplest problem based on these theorems.

These cognitive handicaps are a direct function of the age at which blindness sets in. If blindness does not occur until after

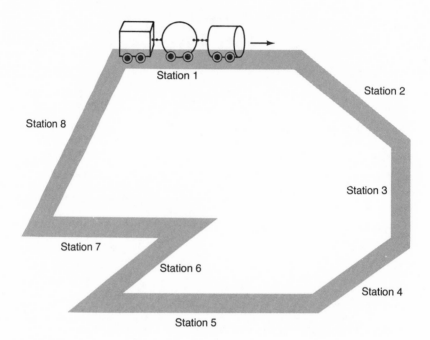

FIGURE 9.5
Congenitally blind children are unable to say which of the three components of this train will arrive at station 2 first. (Data from Hatwell, 1966.)

infancy, the development of spatial concepts is apparently unaffected. Indeed, there was one world-famous geometer who had been blind since the age of three. That much visual experience was enough to ensure that he had the spatial concepts required for discovery and innovation in geometry.[16]

These results are obviously complementary to the results on recovery of visual function after the removal of cataracts. The later the surgical correction, the less likely is the developing organism to be able to deal with the rich array of spatial information that is provided by vision and by no other sense. Habits of dealing with information in a temporal way seem to block the possibility of using spatial information at all. Whether this could be ameliorated by providing the baby with the kind of ultrasonic sensing system described in Chapter 5 is something that we cannot at present discuss, since we lack the relevant information.

The Processes of Development
in Infancy

Why is it that experience in infancy has such potent irreversible consequences in perceptual and cognitive development while at the same time seeming to have rather weaker
effects on personality development, effects that in some cases
are evidently reversible?

A comparison of these two cases brings us to the heart of
the problem of what development is. What is happening when a
child is developing? Infancy is the period in which a lot of development occurs, and occurs at a rapid rate. What does infancy
tell us about the nature of development? At the very outset two
opposed concepts of development were discussed, the nativist
concept and the empiricist concept. These two theories differ in
their view of the role of inputs from the environment in producing developmental advances. According to extreme nativists,
environmental inputs are irrelevant to development; according
to extreme empiricists no development will occur without
specific inputs.

Throughout this book I have been emphasizing the importance of inputs from the environment. I have emphasized the
strength of the empiricist case. Nonetheless, I feel that we must
acknowledge that a modified combination of the two positions is
more likely to be correct. For example, it is clear for some aspects of development that absence of normal inputs from the
environment does not prevent development. Rather, what happens is that development does occur, but it takes an abnormal path.

The development of concepts of space illustrates this, I
think. The sighted infant, exposed from birth to an ordered
three-dimensional world, develops concepts of space that incor-
porate that essential three-dimensionality. The blind infant,
never receiving these inputs, does not stick with the spatial concepts of the newborn. Instead he develops a way of structuring
spatial events in terms of time, a one-dimensional system of
knowing. From the data mentioned above, it is clear that the
choice of a temporal coding of space makes it impossible to
switch back or switch over to the 'normal' three-dimensional

code even if sight is restored. Similarly, a child who has gone for two years down the three-dimensional path will not switch over to the temporal code even if sight is lost.

This surely implies that the developmental process, in this case, at least, is not a passive state, requiring triggers from the environment for anything to occur. Rather, it indicates that the developing organism is seeking ways to organize the world as it is presented to him, and will organize it in terms of whatever information is available. Once a particular line of organization is chosen, specific triggers from the environment may be required to push the process along to its limits, as we saw in Chapter 7. However, some organizing will take place on the basis of any input at all. Its nature will reflect the nature of the structure that is present in the input to the baby. The organization that develops at that point will then determine the kinds of organization that are possible later.

The perceptual and cognitive effects we have discussed result from total loss of the relevant sensory input. Thus there is no opportunity either to utilize this sensory input in central structures or to behave in response to it. The corresponding case does not exist in personality development. *Personality* refers to our repertoires for dealing with people. The newborn not only is ready to deal with people, but must also have people to deal with. Otherwise he will die. In that sense the degree of deprivation possible in personality development is limited. If it were to approach the severity of the loss of sensory input that occurs in blindness, the baby would have no means of surviving. Thus any condition of rearing, no matter how deprived it might seem, must of necessity allow the baby to exercise and develop his inbuilt repertoire of behaviors for coping with people, albeit to a relatively low level.

To compare cognitive development and personality development under conditions of deprivation, we cannot fairly compare the effects of total absence in one case and minimal input in the other. We must compare the effects of minimal inputs with the effects of minimal inputs. Unlike personality development, cognitive development seems able to get along with very minimal inputs, provided they are the right inputs. However, just as the absence of vision can produce a specific, if broad, set of deficits, so we might expect the absence of other specific inputs to produce other quite specific inabilities. Some of the specific inputs have been described in the preceding chapters. The bulk of them remain to be discovered.

Raising a Brighter Baby

At this point in social history there is a widespread interest in attempts to specify the best environment for a baby. In the past, "mother nature," operating through "mother love," was supposed to take care of the process automatically. Now, due to social and economic pressures, many babies are spending time away from their mothers. Many mothers, responding to the competitive pressures of society, are doing the best they can to raise a brighter baby, one better able to cope with the intellectual demands of the educational system that is seen as the key to success, and even survival, in the system. There are also many who have foresaken the system and developed alternative life styles, with alternative patterns of child rearing, the effects of which are only just beginning to be studied.

Is it possible to characterize an environment as "good" or "bad" for a baby? Certain environments are obviously bad. Any environment with minimum social contact, minimal opportunity for exercise, and few or no problem-solving situations is clearly not beneficial for development. However, continuing increments of social contact, exercise opportunities, and the like, does not necessarily imply continuing increments in the "goodness" of the environment.

Two consequences of overburdening a baby's learning capacity have already been mentioned. Too much practice, for example, can automatize a behavior to such an extent that the same behavior cannot be applied in a new situation. A simple instance of this is found in reaching skills. If a baby is put in a situation where an object is always in the same place and can always be reached by the same movement, the baby will stereotypically produce the same movement every time the object is present. He will also produce the same movement in attempting to reach for another object put in a different place.

This kind of stereotyped response can be very readily corrected. However, some of the other areas of development cannot be so easily modified. Stereotyping at any of the stages of concept development seems to introduce developmental delays of many months.

Another hazard of an overenriched environment is the possibility of presenting the baby with more than he can cope with. It seems that babies do enjoy problem solving, but problems that are beyond their resources simply have the opposite effect. The baby retreats from the problem situation completely. No problems to solve and problems too difficult to solve are probably about equally bad from a baby's point of view.

All the above is terribly vague—or perhaps general would be a better word. The best environment for a given individual baby cannot be prescribed in general terms. What is good for a particular baby depends on his overall level of development— social, perceptual, motor, and intellectual. The best we can do is use a schedule of typical development in each of these areas as an index of what the normal baby can do at different ages. This can be used to assess the harmony of development and to judge what kind of inputs are appropriate or necessary, to make sure the baby is neither bored nor frustrated, but rather has an environment which will just challenge his developing competences to grow to their fullest possible limits.

Notes

Chapter 1

1. Erikson, 1950, p. 249.
2. *Ibid.*, pp. 253–254.
3. Fantz, 1961.
4. McCaffrey, 1972.
5. Aronson and Rosenbloom, 1971; Lyons, 1975.
6. Wolff, 1969*a*.

Chapter 2

1. Lipsitt, 1969.
2. Siqueland and Lipsitt, 1966.
3. Wertheimer, 1961.
4. Bower, Broughton, and Moore, 1970*a*.
5. Ball and Tronick, 1971.
6. Dunkeld and Bower, 1976*a*.
7. Bower, 1972; Bower, Broughton, and Moore, 1970*b*.
8. Maratos, 1973; Dunkeld, 1976; Melzoff and Moore, 1975.
9. Bowlby, 1969.
10. Condon, 1975.
11. Birdwhistell, 1970.
12. Condon and Sander, 1974.
13. Condon, 1975.
14. Stott, 1962*a*.
15. Carpenter, 1975.
16. Sander, 1969.

Chapter 3

1. Wolff, 1963.
2. Dittrichova, 1969, p. 165.
3. Ahrens, 1954.
4. Schaffer, 1971.
5. Dennis, 1938.
6. Bower, 1966a; Lipsitt, 1969; Watson, 1966a.
7. Watson, 1973.
8. Papousek, 1969.
9. Hunt and Uzgiris, 1964.
10. Watson, 1973.
11. Bower, 1976a.
12. Watson, 1973, p. 339.
13. Watson, 1966a.
14. Washburn, 1929.

Chapter 4

1. Carpenter, 1975.
2. Ambrose, 1961.
3. Brody and Axelrad, 1971.
4. Anderson, 1972.
5. Schaffer and Emerson, 1964.
6. Spitz, 1950.
7. Schaffer and Emerson, 1964.
8. Schaffer, 1971.
9. Robertson, 1962.
10. Freud and Dann, 1951.
11. Trevarthen, 1975.
12. Schachter, 1959.
13. Schaffer, 1971.
14. Wahler, 1967.
15. Schaffer, 1963.
16. Call, 1975.
17. Freedman and Freedman, 1969.
18. Kringlen and Jorgerson, 1975.
19. Goldberg and Lewis, 1969.
20. Money, 1965.

Chapter 5

1. Dunkeld and Bower, 1976b.
2. Bower, Broughton, and Moore, 1970b, 1970c.
3. Bower and Wishart, 1973.

4. Bower, Broughton, and Moore, 1970*a*.
5. Bower, 1971.
6. Day and McKenzie, 1973.
7. Bower, 1966*a*.
8. McDonnell, 1975; Dunkeld and Bower, 1976*c*.
9. Bower, 1966*b*.
10. Bower and Wishart, 1973.
11. Urwin, 1973.
12. Uhthoff, 1892, p. 91.
13. Wiesel, 1975; Gaze, 1970.

Chapter 6

1. Dennis, 1940.
2. André-Thomas and Dargassies, 1952; Zelazo, Zelazo, and Kolb, 1972.
3. Lenneberg, 1967; McNeill, 1966.
4. Gesell and Thompson, 1929.
5. Bower, 1973; Bruner and Koslowski, 1972.
6. Bower, 1973.
7. White and Held, 1966.
8. Adelson and Fraiberg, 1974.
9. Freedman, 1964.
10. Bower and Wishart, 1973.
11. Held and Hein, 1963.
12. Burlingham, 1961.
13. Supa, Cotzin, and Dallenbach, 1944; Cotzin and Dallenbach, 1950.
14. Bower, Watson, Umansky, and Magoun, 1976.
15. Rynders, 1975.
16. Watson, 1976.

Chapter 7

1. Papousek, 1969.
2. Monnier, 1976.
3. Bower, 1971.
4. Moore, 1975.
5. Mundy-Castle and Anglin, 1969.
6. Piaget, 1937; de Schönen, 1975; Brown and Bower, 1976; Bresson, 1976.
7. Piaget, 1936; Monnier, 1971.
8. Bruner, 1968.
9. Bower and Wishart, 1976.
10. Greenfield, Nelson, and Salzman, 1972.
11. Mounoud and Bower, 1974.

12. Wishart and Bower, 1976*a*; Bever, Mehler, and Epstein, 1968.
13. Gouin-Décarie, 1969.
14. In Bower, 1976.
15. Bower and Paterson, 1972; Wishart and Bower, 1976*b*.

Chapter 8

1. Eimas, Siqueland, Jusczyk, and Vigorito, 1971.
2. Condon and Sander, 1974.
3. Lenneberg, 1967; McNeill, 1966.
4. Lenneberg, 1969.
5. Halliday, 1975, pp. 19–21.
6. Wolff, 1969*b*, p. 98.
7. *Ibid.*, pp. 104–105.

Chapter 9

1. Kringlen and Jorgerson, 1975.
2. Bowlby, 1951.
3. Lorenz, 1952.
4. Harlow, 1959.
5. Bowlby, Ainsworth, Boston, and Rosenbluth, 1956; Beres and Obers, 1950; Rutter, 1972.
6. Freud and Dann, 1951.
7. Schaffer, 1963.
8. Rutter, 1972.
9. Curtiss, Fromkin, Krashen, Rigler, and Rigler, 1974.
10. Money, 1965.
11. Sears, Maccoby, and Levin, 1957.
12. Wiesel, 1975.
13. Drever, 1955; Hatwell, 1966.
14. O'Connor and Hermelin, 1972.
15. Drever, 1962.
16. Drever, 1955.

Bibliography

Adelson, E., and Fraiberg, S.
    1974   Gross motor development in infants blind from birth. *Child Development*, **45**, 114–126.

Ahrens, R.
    1954   Beitrage zur Entvicklung des Physiognomie—und Mimikerkennes. *Zeitschrift für experimentelle und angewardte Psychologie*, **2.**

Ambrose, J. A.
    1961   The development of the smiling response in early infancy. In B. M. Foss (Ed.), *Determinants of infant behaviour*. New York: Wiley.

Anderson, J. W.
    1972   Attachment behaviour out of doors. In N. G. Blurton-Jones (Ed.), *Ethological studies of child behaviour*. London: Cambridge University Press.

André-Thomas and Dargassies, St. A.
    1952   *Etudes neurologique sur le nouveau-né et le jeune nourrisson*. Paris: Masson.

Aronson, E., and Rosenbloom, S.
    1971   Space perception in early infancy: perception within a common auditory-visual space. *Science*, **172**, 1161–1163.

Ball, W., and Tronick, E.
    1971   Infant responses to impending collision: optical and real. *Science*, **171**, 818–820.

Beres, D., and Obers, S. J.
    1950   The effects of extreme deprivation in infancy on psychic structure in adolescence: a study in ego development. *Psychoanalytic Study of the Child*, **5**, 212–235.

Bever, T. G., Mehler, J., and Epstein, J.
    1968   What children do in spite of what they know. *Science*, **162**, 921–924.

Birdwhistell, R. L.
    1970   *Kinesics and context*. Philadelphia: University of Pennsylvania Press.

Bower, T. G. R.
    1966*a*   The visual world of infants. *Scientific American*, **215**, 80–92 (Offprint 502).

Bower, T. G. R.
    1966*b*   Heterogeneous summation in human infants. *Animal Behaviour*, **14**, 395–398.

Bower, T. G. R.
    1971   The object in the world of the infant. *Scientific American*, **225**, 30–38 (Offprint 539).

Bower, T. G. R.
    1972   Object perception in infants. *Perception*, **1**, 15–30.

Bower, T. G. R.
    1973   The development of reaching in infants. Unpublished manuscript, University of Edinburgh.

Bower, T. G. R.
    1974   *Development in infancy*. San Francisco: Freeman.

Bower, T. G. R.
    1976   Notion de l'objet: les yeux, les mains et les paroles. In H. Hécaen (Ed.), *De la motricité à la geste*. Paris: Presses Universitaires de France.

Bower, T. G. R., Broughton, J. M., and Moore, M. K.
    1970*a*   Infant responses to approaching objects: an indicator of response to distal variables. *Perception and Psychophysics*, **9**, 193–196.

Bower, T. G. R., Broughton, J. M., and Moore, M. K.
    1970*b*   Demonstration of intention in the reaching behavior of neonate humans. *Nature*, **228**, 5172.

Bower, T. G. R., Broughton, J. M., and Moore, M. K.
    1970*c*   The coordination of visual and tactual input in infancy. *Perception and Psychophysics*, **8**, 51–53.

Bower, T. G. R., and Paterson, J. G.
    1972   Stages in the development of the object concept. *Cognition*, **1**, 47–55.

Bower, T. G. R., Watson, J. S., Umansky, R., and Magoun, M.
    1976   Auditory surrogates for vision in sensory-motor development. Manuscript submitted for publication.

Bower, T. G. R., and Wishart, J. G.
1973   Development of auditory-manual coordination. Unpublished manuscript, University of Edinburgh.

Bower, T. G. R., and Wishart, J. G.
1976   Compensation and conservation in the drinking behaviour of infants. Unpublished manuscript, University of Edinburgh.

Bowlby, J.
1951   *Maternal care and mental health.* Geneva: World Health Organization.

Bowlby, J.
1969   *Attachment and loss:* Vol. 1, *Attachment.* London: Hogarth.

Bowlby, J., Ainsworth, M. D., Boston, M., and Rosenbluth, D.
1956   The effects of mother-child separation: a follow-up study. *British Journal of Medical Psychology,* **29**, 211–247.

Bresson, F., Maury, L., Pieraut-Bonniec, G., and de Schönen, S.
1976   Organisation and lateralization of reaching in infants: an instance of asymmetric functions in hand collaboration. *Neuropsychologia* (in press).

Brody, J., and Axelrad, S.
1971   Maternal stimulation and the social responsiveness of infants. In H. R. Schaffer (Ed.), *The origins of human social relations.* London: Academic Press.

Brown, I. E., and Bower, T. G. R.
1976   The problem of object permanence. *Cognition* (in press).

Bruner, J. S.
1968   *Processes of cognitive growth: infancy.* Worcester, Mass.: Clark University Press.

Bruner, J. S., and Koslowski, B.
1972   Visually preadapted constituents of manipulatory action. *Perception,* **1**, 3–15.

Burlingham, D.
1961   Some notes on the development of the blind. *Psychoanalytic Study of the Child,* **62**, 121–145.

Call, J.
1975   Paper presented at meeting of the Southern California Psychiatric Association, Los Angeles.

Carpenter, G.
1975   Mother's face and the newborn. In R. Lewin (Ed.), *Child alive.* London: Temple Smith.

Condon, W. S.
1975   Speech makes babies move. In R. Lewin (Ed.), *Child alive.* London: Temple Smith.

Condon, W. S., and Sander, L.
    1974   Neonate movement is synchronized with adult speech: in-
            teractional participation and language acquisition. *Sci-
            ence*, **183**, 99–101.

Cotzin, M., and Dallenbach, K. M.
    1950   "Facial vision": the role of pitch and loudness in the per-
            ception of obstacles by the blind. *American Journal of Psy-
            chology*, **63**, 485–515.

Curtiss, S., Fromkin, V., Krashen, S., Rigler, D., and Rigler, M.
    1974   The linguistic development of Genie. *Language*, **50**, 528–
            554.

Day, R. H., and McKenzie, B. E.
    1973   Perceptual shape constancy in early infancy. *Perception*, **2**,
            315–321.

Dennis, W.
    1938   Infant development under conditions of restricted practice
            and of minimum social stimulation: a preliminary report.
            Journal of Genetic Psychology, **53**, 149–158.

Dennis, W.
    1940   The effect of cradling practices upon the onset of walking
            in Hopi children. *Journal of Genetic Psychology*, **56**, 77–86.

de Schönen, S.
    1975   Report for Le Centre pour l'Etude de la Pensée et le Lan-
            gage, Ecole Practique des Hautes Etudes, Paris.

Dittrichova, J.
    1969   In R. J. Robinson (Ed.), *Brain and early behaviour*. London:
            Academic Press.

Drever, J.
    1955   Early learning and the perception of space. *American
            Journal of Psychology*, **68**, 605–614.

Drever, J.
    1962   Perception in action. *Bulletin of the British Psychological
            Society*, **45**, 1–14.

Dunkeld, J.
    1976   The development of imitation in infancy. Doctoral disser-
            tation, University of Edinburgh.

Dunkeld, J., and Bower, T. G. R.
    1976a   Infant response to impending optical collision. Manuscript
            submitted for publication.

Dunkeld, J., and Bower, T. G. R.
    1976b   Intersensory differentiation in infancy. Unpublished man-
            uscript, University of Edinburgh.

Dunkeld, J., and Bower, T. G. R.
1976c The effect of wearing prisms on reaching behaviour. Unpublished manuscript, University of Edinburgh.

Eimas, P. D., Siqueland, E. R., Jusczyk, P., and Vigorito, J.
1971 Speech perception in infants. *Science*, **171**, 303–306.

Erikson, E. H.
1950 *Childhood and society*. New York: Norton; London: The Hogarth Press.

Fantz, R. L.
1961 The origin of form perception. *Scientific American*, **204**, 66–72 (Offprint 459).

Freedman, D. G.
1964 Smiling in blind infants and the issue of innate versus acquired. *Journal of Child Psychology and Psychiatry and Allied Disciplines*, **5**, 171–184.

Freedman, D. G., and Freedman, N. C.
1969 Sensory capabilities: attention, indicator responses. *Nature*, **224**, 1227.

Freud, A., and Dann, S.
1951 An experiment in group upbringing. *Psychoanalytic Study of the Child*, **6**, 127–168.

Gaze, R. M.
1970 *The formation of nerve connections*. London: Academic Press.

Gesell, A., and Thompson, H.
1929 Learning and growth in identical infant twins: an experimental study by the method of co-twin control. *Genetic Psychology Monographs*, **6**, 1–125.

Gibson, J. J.
1950 *The perception of the visual world*. Boston: Houghton Mifflin.

Goldberg, S., and Lewis, M.
Play behavior in the year-old infant: early sex differences. *Child Development*, **40**, 21–32.

Gouin-Décarie, T.
1969 A study of the mental and emotional development of the thalidomide child. In B. M. Foss (Ed.), *Determinants of infant behaviour*, Vol. 4. London: Methuen.

Greenfield, P. M., Nelson, K., and Salzman, E.
1972 The development of rulebound strategies for manipulating seriated cups: a parallel between action and grammar. *Cognitive Psychology*, **3**, 291–310.

Halliday, M. A. K.
　　1973　*Explorations in the functions of language*. London: Arnold.
Halliday, M. A. K.
　　1975　*Learning how to mean: explorations in the development of language*. London: Arnold.
Harlow, H. F.
　　1959　Love in infant monkeys. *Scientific American*, **200**, 68–74 (Offprint 429).
Hatwell, Y.
　　1966　*Privation sensorielle et intelligence*. Paris: Presses Universitaires de France.
Held, R.
　　1965　Plasticity in sensory-motor systems. *Scientific American*, **213**, 84–94 (Offprint 494).
Held, R., and Hein, A.
　　1963　Movement-produced stimulation in the development of visually guided behavior. *Journal of Comparative Physiology and Psychology*, **37**, 87–95.
Hubel, D. H., and Wiesel, T. N.
　　1962　Receptive fields, binocular interaction, and functional architecture in the cat's visual cortex. *Journal of Physiology*, **160**, 106–156.
Hunt, J. McV., and Uzgiris, I. C.
　　1964　Cathexis from recognitive familiarity: an exploratory study. Paper presented at convention of the American Psychological Association, Los Angeles.
Kringlen, E., and Jorgerson, K.
　　1975　Personality development in twins. Unpublished manuscript, Center for Advanced Study in the Behavioral Sciences, Stanford University.
Lenneberg, E. H.
　　1964　Speech as a motor skill with special reference to non-aphasic disorders. *Child Development Monographs*, **29**, 115–126.
Lenneberg, E. H.
　　1967　*Biological foundations of language*, New York: Wiley.
Lenneberg, E. H.
　　1969　On explaining language. *Science*, **164**, 635–643.
Lipsitt, L.
　　1969　Learning capacities of the human infant. In R. J. Robinson (Ed.), *Brain and early behaviour*. London: Academic Press.

Lorenz, K.
1952   *King Solomon's ring.* London: Methuen.

Lyons, K.
1975   Integration of auditory and visual spatial information in early infancy. Paper presented at Conference of the Society for Research in Child Development, Denver.

McCaffrey, A.
1972   Doctoral dissertation, Cornell University.

McDonnell, P.
1975   The development of visually guided reaching. *Perception and Psychophysics,* **18**, 181–185.

McNeill, D.
1966   Developmental psycholinguistics. In F. Smith and G. A. Miller (Eds.), *The genesis of language.* Cambridge, Mass.: M.I.T. Press.

Maratos, O.
1973   The origin and development of imitation in the first six months of life. Doctoral dissertation, University of Geneva.

Melzoff, A., and Moore, M. K.
1975   Paper presented at conference of the Society for Research in Child Development, Denver.

Money, J.
1965   Psychosexual differentiation. In J. Money (Ed.), *Sex research: new developments.* New York: Holt, Rinehart & Winston.

Monnier, C.
1971   Report of the Centre d'Epistemologie Génétique, Geneva.

Monnier, C.
1976   La genèse de l'experimentation: exploration d'objets nouveaux par les bébés. Doctoral dissertation. University of Geneva.

Moore, M. K.
1975   Object permanence and object identity. Paper presented at conference of the Society for Research in Child Development, Denver.

Mounoud, P., and Bower, T. G. R.
1974   Conservation of weight in infants. *Cognition,* **3**, 29–40.

Mundy-Castle, A. C., and Anglin, J.
1969   The development of looking in infancy. Paper presented at conference of the Society for Research in Child Development, Santa Monica, Calif.

O'Connor, N., and Hermelin, B.
   1972   Seeing and hearing in space and time. *Perception and Psychophysics*, **11**, 46–48.

Papousek, H.
   1969   Individual variability in learned responses in human infants. In R. J. Robinson (Ed.), *Brain and early behaviour*. London: Academic Press.

Piaget, J.
   1954   *Origins of intelligence*. New York: Basic Books (original French edition, 1936).

Piaget, J.
   1955   *The construction of reality in the child*. London: Routledge & Kegan Paul (original French edition, 1937).

Robertson, J. (Ed.)
   1972   *Hospitals and children: a parent's eye view*. London: Gollancz.

Rutter, M.
   1972   *Maternal deprivation reassessed*. Harmondsworth, England: Penguin.

Rynders, J.
   1975   *Annual Report of the University of Minnesota Institute of Child Development*.

Sander, L. W.
   1969   Regulation and organisation in the early infant-caretaker system. In R. J. Robinson (Ed.), *Brain and early behaviour*. London: Academic Press.

Schachter, S.
   1959   *The psychology of affiliation*. Stanford, Calif.: Stanford University Press.

Schaffer, H. R.
   1963   Some issues for research in the study of attachment behaviour. In B. M. Foss (Ed.), *Determinants of infant behaviour*, Vol. 2. New York, Wiley.

Schaffer, H. R.
   1971   *The growth of sociability*. Harmondsworth, England: Penguin.

Schaffer, H. R., and Emerson, P. E.
   1964   The development of social attachments in infancy. *Monographs of the Scoiety for Research in Child Development*, **29**, 3.

Sears, R. R., Maccoby, E. E., and Levin, H.
   1957   *Patterns of child rearing*. New York: Harper & Row.

Shirley, M. M.
    1959   *The first two years, Vol. I: Postural and locomotor developments*. Minneapolis: University of Minnesota Press.

Siqueland, E. R., and Lipsitt, L. P.
    1966   Conditioned head-turning in human newborns. *Journal of Experimental Child Psychology*, **3**, 356–376.

Spitz, R. A.
    1950   Anxiety in infancy: a study of its manifestations in the first year of life. *International Journal of Psychoanalysis*, **31**, 138–143.

Spitz, R. A., and Wolf, K. M.
    1946   The smiling response: a contribution to the ontogenesis of social relations. *Genetic Psychology Monographs*, **34**, 57–125.

Stott, D. H.
    1959   Evidence for prenatal impairment of temperament in mentally subnormal children. *Vita Humana*, **2**, 125–148.

Stott, D. H.
    1962*a* Abnormal mothering as a cause of mental subnormality, I: A critique of some classic studies of maternal deprivation in the light of possible congenital factors. *Journal of Child Psychology and Psychiatry and Allied Disciplines*, **3**, 79–93.

Stott, D. H.
    1962*b* Abnormal mothering as a cause of mental subnormality, II. *Journal of Child Psychology and Psychiatry and Allied Disciplines*, **3**, 133–148.

Supa, M., Cotzin, M., and Dallenbach, K. M.
    1944   "Facial vision": the perception of obstacles by the blind. *American Journal of Psychology*, **57**, 133–183.

Trevarthen, C.
    1975   *Early attempts at speech*. In R. Lewin (Ed.), *Child alive*. London: Temple Smith.

Uhthoff, D. D.
    1960   Helmholtz-Festschrift Z.70 Geburtstag. In M. von Senden, *Space and sight*. London: Methuen (original German edition, 1891).

Urwin, C.
    1973   The development of a blind baby. Unpublished manuscript read at University of Edinburgh, January.

von Hofsten, C.
    1976   Binocular convergence as a determinant in reaching behaviour in infancy. *Perception* (in press).

Wahler, R. G.
1967 Infant social attachments: a reinforcement theory interpretation and investigation. *Child Development,* **38,** 1079–1088.

Washburn, R. W.
1929 A study of smiling and laughing of infants in the first year of life. *Genetic Psychology Monographs,* **6,** 396–537.

Watson, J. S.
1966a Perception of object orientation in infants. *Merrill-Palmer Quarterly of Behaviour and Development,* **12,** 73–94.

Watson, J. S.
1966b The development and generalisation of "contingency awareness" in early infancy: some hypotheses. *Merrill-Palmer Quarterly of Behaviour and Development,* **12,** 123–135.

Watson, J. S.
1973 Smiling, cooing and "the game." *Merrill-Palmer Quarterly of Behaviour and Development,* **18,** 323–339.

Wertheimer, M.
1961 Psycho-motor coordination of auditory-visual space at birth. *Science,* **134,** 1692.

White, B., and Held, R.
1966 Plasticity of sensory-motor development in the human infant. In J. F. Rosenblith and W. Allinsmith (Eds.), *The causes of behavior.* Boston: Allyn & Bacon.

Wiesel, T. N.
1975 Grass Foundation Lectures, Stanford University.

Wishart, J. G., and Bower, T. G. R.
1976a The development of number conservation in infancy. Unpublished manuscript, University of Edinburgh.

Wishart, J. G., and Bower, T. G. R.
1976b Comprehension of spatial relations in the development of the object concept. Unpublished manuscript, University of Edinburgh.

Wolff, P. H.
1963 Observations on the early development of smiling. In B. M. Foss (Ed.), *Determinants of infant behaviour,* Vol. 2. New York: Wiley.

Wolff, P. H.
1969a Motor development and holotencephaly. In R. J. Robinson (Ed.), *Brain and early behaviour.* London: Academic Press.

Wolff, P. H.
   1969*b* The natural history of crying and other vocalisations in
           early infancy. In B. M. Foss (Ed.), *Determinants of infant
           behaviour*, Vol. 4. London: Methuen.

Zelazo, P. R., Zelazo, N. A., and Kolb, S.
   1972   "Walking" in the newborn. *Science*, **176**, 314–315.

Index

Ability, innate vs. acquired, 16
Absolutism, 119–120, 123
Adelson, E., 96n, 171
Affectionless character, 151, 152, 154
Age
  chronological, 38
  conceptual, 38
  and separation anxiety, 58
Ambrose, J. A., 50, 171
Anglin, J., 112, 171
Anthropologist, 6–7
Anxiety, separation, 50–55, 58
Apathy, 51. *See also* Passivity
Aronson, E., 11, 171
Arrhinencephaly, 13
Association, 143
Associative learning, 53
Attachment, 35, 49–66
  and ability to learn, 60
  artificial, 151
  child-child, 54–55
  communication theory of, 55–61
  deprivation, 155
  and institutionalization, 155
  and loss, 150, 156
  multiple, 156
  and personality development, 151–157
Attentional capacity, 73–80, 83
Attentiveness, social, 55
Auditory localization, 18
Azimuth position, 97, 99, 102

Basic mistrust, 2
Basic trust, 2, 3, 4
Behavior
  egocentric, 119
  nonverbal, 143
Behavioral disturbance, 150
Binocular vision, 85, 159
Bit, 77, 78
Blindness, 83, 158, 160, 161, 163
  congenital, 84, 160, 161
  and echo, 102–105
  and motor development, 94–105, 149
Block manipulation, 91
Body movement, 30, 31
Bower, T. G. R., 18n, 21n, 25n, 26n, 71n, 74n, 75n, 80n, 82n, 83n, 114n, 127n, 129n, 143n, 172, 173, 180
Bruner, J. S., 120, 173

Camera, 48
Carpenter, G., 34, 173
Cataract, 159, 162
Chronological age, 38
Circular tracking, 128
Cognitive development, 107–131, 160, 164
  mechanisms of, 123–131
  and smiling, 41–48
Communication, 5–6, 30, 34
  development of skills in, 31
  disturbances in, 31

184 / Index